David Hanks

CHELTENHAM
PAST & PRESENT

DAVID HANKS

The
History
Press

First published 2010

The History Press
The Mill, Brimscombe Port
Stroud, Gloucestershire, GL5 2QG
www.thehistorypress.co.uk

British Library Cataloguing in Publication Data.
A catalogue record for this book is available from the British Library.

ISBN 978 0 7524 5366 8

Typesetting and origination by The History Press
Printed in Great Britain

BRITISH BOOKSHOPS AND STATIONERS
101 High Street
Cheltenham
Gloucs
GL50 1DP

07-02-11 14:26   SALE   2 4805   959
PRODUCT   QTY   £   V

CHELTENHAM PAST & PRESEN 1   7.99

    TOTAL   1   7.99
    CASH   10.00
    TOTAL TENDERED   10.00
    CHANGE   2.01

Tax Summary	Goods	Tax
2=VAT 0.00	7.99	0.00

CONTENTS

ACKNOWLEDGEMENTS

In addition to pictures from my own collection, I am grateful to the following people who kindly supplied copies. Within this like-minded group I have come across some extremely knowledgeable and helpful individuals, including erudite local historians and avid collectors, willing to share their knowledge and exchange pictures, thereby expanding our collective understanding of this town's complex past. They include: the Frith Collection for reproduction of the picture on p. 69 from a postcard in the author's collection, Rick Kedge, Ron Prewer, Freda Gittos, Terry Sims, Pat Pearce, Dawn Hulbert, Mike Mitchell, Brian Torode, David Butler, John Milner, Pat Johnson, Garth Martin, Elaine and Geoffrey North, Joe Stevens, Steven Blake, Patsy Langmead, Rachel Roberts, Alan Gill, Tom and Juliet Barnes, Ken Ward and last, but not least, Annie Hanks, with sincere apologies to anyone I have overlooked. This project was completed as Dr Steven Blake set out for Australia to follow in the footsteps of George Rowe, Cheltenham's most famous nineteenth-century printmaker. Particular thanks go to Steven, who will I am sure eventually find himself recorded as Cheltenham's most acclaimed twentieth-century local historian.

INTRODUCTION

'Cheltenham, alias Chilteham alias Cheltham, is a Towne situated on ye north side of a small purling Silver Stream or Rivulet called Chilt . . . It is an ancient Market Towne . . . which is one Street continued with the buildings on each side for a full mile in length . . . Albeit not a Corporation, yet it is a very ancient Burrough abounding in Sundry Privileges. . . .'

This is part of the first known attempt to write a brief history of Cheltenham in the 1692 Manor Court records by John Prinn[1] – unfortunately without pictures. Beyond the few later paintings and engravings in this introduction we will be looking at some of Cheltenham's nineteenth- and early twentieth-century photographs to see how they saw this 'one street with buildings on each side', two centuries after Mr Prinn penned his short seventeenth-century description of the town.

Cheltenham from Leckhampton Hill on a *c.* 1840 lithograph by George Rowe. St Peter's Church, Leckhampton, is lower left, Tower Lodge is in the foreground and the new (1840) Christchurch, is in the centre distance.

---

1. For more about John Prinn see www.charlton-park-cheltenham.co.uk and the online e-book.

Firstly we will try to answer the question 'When, where and in what sort of conditions were the earliest photographs of Cheltenham taken?' Compared with other similar-sized towns, Cheltenham's first photographs were taken surprisingly early, anytime between the 1840s and 1900s, with the earliest street scenes captured between the middle and close of the nineteenth century. Today an almost insatiable quest for pictorial history finds us peering back through a small aperture-keyhole at any surviving views. My interest in Cheltenham's photographic heritage prompted a window display in a High Street shop in 2007 of some early photographs. Feedback suggested they be published for future enjoyment and preservation, the alternative being they might not surface again for wider enjoyment, like some other local pictures I know of.

Stepping back to the eighteenth century to see how this 'apparently healthy', embryonic spa town was evolving, we need to try to balance things a little by showing that all was not necessarily as it appeared to be. This was the period during which a few of Cheltenham's earliest surviving (non-photographic) views were created, as artists and printmakers set up shop, producing and selling paintings, sketches, engravings and lithographs. Such depictions of Cheltenham that survive today reflect varying degrees of accuracy and the phrase 'artistic licence' is sometimes appropriate to explain how an individual's personal interpretation of street scenes contained minor deviations of content or perspective when comparing their still-valuable work with the less disputable photography that followed a century later.

A painting of Cheltenham High Street popularly thought to be from about 1740. The old Plough Inn Tavern on the left was sold in 1795 and advertised having a frontage of 105ft, stabling for 100 horses, and granaries for 5,000 bushels of wheat. *(Picture courtesy of Cheltenham Art Gallery & Museum)*

Early in the following century, still some fifty years before any street photographs, a noted writer described this scene glowingly as: 'the stream flowed down the centre of the High Street until after 1800 and both sides could only be reached by using rude bridges formed of stepping stones. The rural appearance of the whole must have been considerably increased by noble trees which appeared at intervals, partly overhanging the stream, offering their grateful shade to the weary traveller who sought refreshment and vigour from its waters.'

The Chelt needed to be redirected several times a week from Cambray Mill Pond to clean the foul High Street and this was begrudgingly done by the miller. Following this painting, significant changes followed, including the filling-in of the channel of the stream, the demolition of the Market House, Butter Cross and Gaol in the centre of the street, the installation of a 4½ft stone pavement and 120 erratic gas lamps along the street.

I said 'apparently healthy' because from these descriptions it is easy to envisage an almost idyllic, semi-rural riparian market town. In reality it was a deceptive view, barely hinting at the hazardous truth lurking behind written descriptions or oil-on-canvas depictions of a place unhealthily full of privies and pigsties, the other half of which was actively promoting it to attract visitors and residents to its new spas, not deter them. So here we must add a little balance, particularly in relation to the putrid River Chelt, because after joining forces with the River Ham, the more likely consequences of 'seeking refreshment and vigour from the waters' was dire. Until the 1830s Cheltenham's domestic water came mostly from private wells and its only sewers were open brooks and ditches. Following this High Street painting the town's rapidly increasing population continued dumping its waste into the River Chelt and things frequently deteriorated to the point where lurking health hazards (typhus, cholera and smallpox) revealed a more alarming picture of things, even if the General Hospital was just down the street.

Faced with this dilemma, in 1824 a private water company was formed, pumping piped water to a few of the town's larger houses willing to pay for it. By the mid-1830s, at a cost of some £7,600, a total of 5,892 yards of inadequate sewers were installed. Prone to 'exploding' after severe storms, the main one in the High Street was 2,200 yards long and when dug in 1834 the ancient stepping-stones seen in this painting and some massive oak steps were unearthed. The pipe network increasingly struggled to cope as the population grew.[2] By 1849 an enquiry held at the George Hotel in the High Street reported that of some 6,541 houses in the borough, only 736 in 19 nearby streets were served by sewers, with more than 5,000 having no legal outlet. The Chelt was thoroughly polluted and the emptying of sewerage into it from private sewers constituted a public health nuisance, exacerbated by flooding – another dilemma suffered by Cheltenham folk from time immemorial.

A report in 1853 stated: 'Although the town is exceedingly well situated for drainage, and a considerable amount of work for this purpose has been executed . . . much of it appears to be defective. . . . The River Chelt running through the centre of town from East to West, and receiving a large share of its drainage, is in an exceedingly bad state, and has long been a fruitful source of disease and injury. Along its course are three water mills, the dams of which, penning back the foul matters discharged, constitute so many huge open cesspools which in warm weather are intolerable and from which in times of flood the water and filth flow back into the houses, an evil which has occurred three times in six weeks.'

---

2. In 1801 there were 3,076 people in the whole of Cheltenham Hundred. By 1826 there were over 20,000 and by 1851 Cheltenham Parish alone had 35,062 inhabitants in 6,343 houses. There are now over 100,000 inhabitants in Cheltenham.

An 1820s view of the former Plough Inn, now rebuilt as the more upmarket Plough Hotel with daily 'Royal Mails and Light and Elegant Post Coaches' to Gloucester, London and Milford. The 'Berkeley Hunt' coach to London was advertised as leaving at 6 a.m. arriving in London at 4.30 p.m. for dinner. The High Street is cleaner and can be crossed with dry feet, though until the 1850s some 25 cartloads of water were needed daily to keep the dust down. It has stone walkways, basic underground drainage and the twice-weekly sluicing by the redirected Chelt from Cambray Mill pond now appears unnecessary.

George Rowe's *c.* 1840 print of the Plough Hotel, topped with a simple pediment on the central section of its High Street façade and with fourth storey attic rooms brought forward.

More new drainpipes had been installed, which by the 1850s caused a lowering of ground water. Residents were then up in arms after their wells ran dry; water carts were unable to meet the demand and the town urgently needed an efficient water supply. The Town Commissioners (pre-1876 incorporation when the first mayor was appointed) appear to have put their water carts before the horses for some years by installing even more sewerage pipes without a commensurate increase in water supply to ensure it all functioned efficiently. A reliable water supply was essential for many purposes, including domestic use, street cleaning, public baths, fountains, fire-fighting, and of course the numerous hotels and small businesses trying to establish themselves here. All required fresh water and by 1857 the Hewletts Reservoir (16 million gallons) was under construction to try to meet the demand, but it was not until 1866 that Cheltenham's sewerage was disposed of by irrigation, as opposed to dumping, after which things improved greatly. This was also the period during which the ever-innovative Victorians made other environmental improvements, including gas, electricity and better transportation (road and rail) all of which encouraged more people and businesses here – including, of course, the first photographer.

A retrospective description of the old market town penned by George Rowe in the 1840s recalls, 'the image of bygone days when this busy thoroughfare was encumbered with an old Market House . . . and the sandy road of the High Street was occasionally diversified by a patch of stunted grass on which vagrant cattle gathered a scanty meal'. Such rearward glances through rose-tinted optics were probably illusory because the unkempt and unhealthy 'Great Street' of earlier times was often reduced to a quagmire by hooves and wheel rims, and even in drier times needed watering to keep the dust down and swill the filth away. Despite considerable improvements to the old market town's backwater sluicing practices, much as today, some change was accepted, even appreciated, and some not. In 1826 when William Cobbett rode along the town's new and improved, less-fettered High Street he still recorded his personal dislike of things, calling it, 'a nasty, ill-looking place, half clown and half cockney, and of being one street about a mile long'. Some early civic pride may have existed because next time Cobbett ill-advisedly rode into Cheltenham the mob almost lynched him!

This local advertisement (31 August 1841) shows just how quickly Cheltenham established itself on the global photographic scene. The first photographic portrait studio in the world opened in New York in 1840 and Richard Beard opened England's first professional portrait studio in Regent Street, London, in March 1841. He quickly followed this with similar licensed portrait studios in Plymouth, Bristol, Cheltenham, Liverpool, Nottingham, Brighton, Bath and Manchester. Note how most are cities, with the exception of the three spa towns where Mr Beard shrewdly calculated there was good potential for his franchised business network.

NOW OPEN.

PHOTOGRAPHIC INSTITUTION,
IMPERIAL NURSERY, PROMENADE.

By Royal Letters Patent.

THE Nobility, Gentry, and Inhabitants of Cheltenham, Gloucester, and their Vicinities, are respectfully informed, that the above Institution for taking PHOTOGRAPHIC PORTRAITS by the combined Processes of the PHOTOGRAPHIC and DAGUER-REOTYPE Patents, IS NOW OPEN.

These unerring likenesses are produced by the agency of light in a few Seconds, and are as exquisite in detail, as they are undeviating in fidelity to their originals; in both respects they stand pre-eminent over every effort of the human hand. From the improvements recently introduced, the state of the weather offers no impediment to the operation.

A portrait in a neat Morocco Case, may be sent by Post to any part of the Kingdom.

With such descriptive and artistic images in mind, it is time to move forward to the advent of photography – the crux of this publication. By 1840 George Rowe was the most prominent of Cheltenham's artists, printers and lithographers and the first commercial threat to his business was about to arrive, no doubt as he did, by horse or coach-and-horses. It was the cusp of other great developments impacting locally and nationally, including the first passenger trains, replacing local horse-drawn transport after the MR Birmingham & Gloucester line came to Cheltenham-Lansdown in 1840. By 1847 Lansdown station was connected with the closer St James's station. That was when Isambard Kingdom Brunel came to Cheltenham and GWR trains commenced to Stroud, Swindon and London. But in 1841, when the enterprising Mr Palmer arrived from London, he would have used traditional horse drawn transport. George Rowe would soon have heard of this particular newcomer and quietly taken stock of the potential threat posed to his own well-established print business. In September 1841 Mr Palmer opened Cheltenham's first photographic studio. This pioneering Victorian start-up business undoubtedly created a mixture of excitement and consternation and his 'Photographic Institution' was soon attracting brisk business at Imperial Nursery (today's Imperial Gardens) – but whether Mr Palmer had the essential piped water to wash his photographic plates at this particular time we know not.

The local press described this new venture as: 'A Valuable Invention . . . which will, we have no doubt, create much interest in Cheltenham.'

This is something of an understatement compared with modern headlines, and things never looked back. By 1900 there were 18 independent photographic businesses in Cheltenham.

Initially, the going rate for a 'sitting' in Mr Palmer's newly licensed portrait studio was a guinea.[3] If all went well 'sitters' received their 'likeness' as a small Daguerreotype (post-1839) photograph. Some of the early portrait photographs were pasted onto stiff cardboard known as 'Cabinet Cards' (6 x 4 inches) and from 1857 on smaller 'Cartes de Visite' (CDVs) or visiting cards (4 x 2½ inches). From the outset, the Daguerreotype process did not stand still, even though the subjects were expected to. Other evolving types of early monochrome photography included Ambertype and Collodion glass-positive processes, developed, modified and perfected during the 1850s. All employed a combination of chemistry, photographic and artistic skills, as suggested on the 'CDV' view William Suter took of his photographic premises (p. 102). Skilled artists were occasionally employed to add a hint of colour to early photographs for customers who may previously have seen their likeness as a coloured miniature. Eventually, the competitive popularity of photography, hand-tinted or otherwise, together with the camera's accuracy, saw these revolutionary methods of recording people and places supersede the interpretive drawing and painting skills of old. More and more of Cheltenham's wealthier residents and visitors booked sittings in a steadily increasing number of studios where the 'sitter' froze compliantly in front of the camera for a good few seconds, with much slower shutter speeds and less efficient lighting techniques.

Another item in the local press reveals that in 1843, in addition to studio portrait photography, Mr Palmer was increasingly commissioned to photograph 'Villas, Mansions and Buildings generally, including Paintings and Statuary'. This snippet of information is the next best clue as to when Cheltenham's first studio photographer began hauling his comparatively bulky glass-plate rig outside, taking some of Cheltenham's earliest topographical photographs. Exactly when Mr Palmer and other photographers progressed

---

3. A guinea was £1 and 1 shilling, or 21 shillings (£1.05p in decimal currency) equivalent to about £70 today, according to the modern Retail Price Index.

from work in private houses and gardens to capturing random street scenes is unknown, but we may reasonably assume it to have been during the 1850s or 1860s. It was probably done at the photographer's expense, with occasional commissions to photograph streets or buildings. The earliest confirmed date for topographical views in this book is April 1864, no doubt with a few before that date and plenty more after. It is worth mentioning that 1864 was still almost forty years before the commencement of full-front picture postcards (PCs) which became so popular in about 1902, declining almost as rapidly at the outbreak of the First World War, and arguably never recovering their former quality or desirability thereafter.

So while we know that some of Cheltenham's earliest street photographs were taken in the 1860s and thereafter, that's about *all* we know. Nevertheless, it is reasonable to conclude that some of those earliest street views are in this book, coming from a few undated CDVs created from 1857 onwards, when street photography was in its infancy. Albumen CDVs now appear to be one of the most enduring formats preserving a few of our early views and the small number surviving represents an important part of our photographic heritage. Stating that fact here will (hopefully) see a few more local pictures surfacing. CDVs preceded the introduction of (date-stamped if posted) half-fronted picture postcards in the late 1890s. These accomplishments enabled the Victorians to leave behind photographs now anything up to 150 years old, of Elizabethan, Georgian and Victorian Cheltenham before parts were changed or lost. It is easy to sound critical and controversial when describing some of this change, when the intention is to be constructive about what has been preserved, as well as acknowledging justified comments about what has been replaced. Either way, it is still fair to say that some of Cheltenham's architectural alterations veered between necessary improvements at one end of the scale to a questionable desire for modernism at the other. Some of it can, and has been rightly described as destruction and irretrievable loss, the true impact of which you can partially judge for yourselves, as well as other schemes which thankfully did not leave the drawing board, avoiding some equally dubious additions to the town.[4]

Following the advent of the ground-breaking nineteenth-century photography was another product of Victorian ingenuity, and possibly the greatest of all time, the amazing transition after millennia of equine horsepower to mechanical horsepower, when the earliest motor vehicles appeared on Cheltenham streets. I believe this saw the close of what is described as the age of elegance. It was when well-born, horse-borne and horse-drawn Cheltenham folk embraced the exciting new era of motorised combustion – and congestion. Motor transport is conspicuous by its absence in the early photographs, being another twenty or thirty years down the road before modern steam, petrol and electrically propelled contraptions arrived here. Today it is almost impossible to take street photographs without including motor cars. Although the town's electric trams were phased out by 1930, for the time being at least, cars dominate the roads, appearing in almost every photograph.

Unlike old carriages, cars and trams, the loss, alteration or overbuilding of structures is practically irreversible and early photographs now bear silent witness to this. For whatever reason it was decided to remove, redesign or replace some of Cheltenham's buildings, these and other similar photographs now form the only visual record of that particular moment in time, such as the change of porch entrance on the parish church, moved some 45ft to the left by the Victorians (p. 127) or the greater impact of losing St James railway station, or the effect on the High Street of losing two consecutive grammar

---

4. See www.charlton-park-cheltenham.co.uk and go to page 58 of the online e-book: expand the picture of the town from Leckhampton Hill.

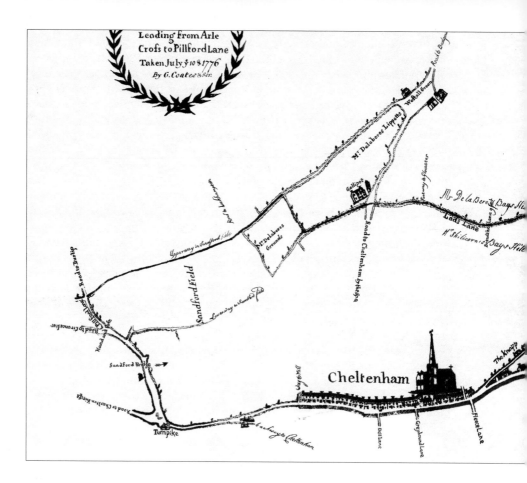

schools (pp. 76–80), numerous hotels, including the Plough, the Royal, the Crown, the George, the Lamb, the Imperial, the York, the Fleece, the Swan and more. Consequently, the passage of time transforms the everyday work of local artists and photographers into a priceless, though fragmentary legacy of gradual and occasionally beneficial change, the posterity value of which is prized by most of us today. The early photographers may well have known what occurred here in the past but they would have had little idea of what was to follow, ranging as it did from airborne bombs to self-interested decisions of developers, of less caring planners, facilitated by encouraging amounts of blinkered civic foresight, or plain oversight.

Oliver Bradbury, in his book *Cheltenham's Lost Heritage* (Sutton Publishing, 2004), and Steven Blake before him, have highlighted better than I the extent of Cheltenham's architectural losses. One sobering fact from Mr Bradbury's book is that of 196 prime buildings illustrated in George Rowe's (pre-photographic) *Cheltenham Illustrated Guide* of 1845 only 88 survived at the turn of the twenty-first century. Such losses suggest this statistic alone be writ large across the white boards of the planning department, and any other bodies influencing future destruction and development plans in this already diminished town. Anyone putting a selection of historic Cheltenham pictures together is inevitably drawn into commenting on the bigger picture they reveal, particularly in relation to the preservation and loss of historic buildings. Built in any of Britain's 'New Towns', some of the post-war developments that bought into Cheltenham might pass

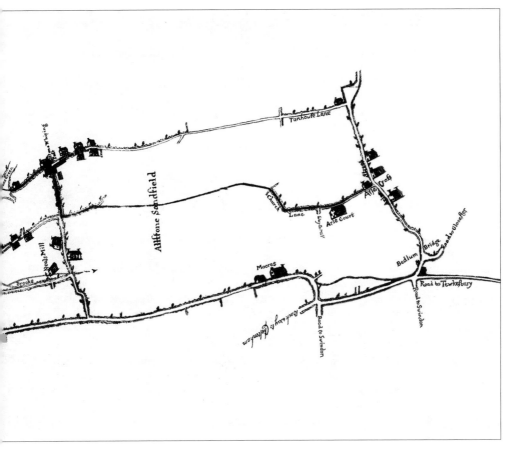

Coates' 1776 map of Cheltenham, with nearby hamlets and farmsteads, 12 years before the 1788 visit of King George III and family, after which the town's Regency expansion took off and the whole disparate area gelled into one. Prior to the eighteenth century, it was known to some by its one-and-a-half-mile street, referred to as The Great Street or simply Cheltenham Street (Leland – 1540s) some of its many off-shoot lanes and alleyways were later widened, becoming streets in their own right. *(Map courtesy of Gloucestershire Archives – Ref QSRH1777A/1)*

without comment. But where such contemporary designs are imposed on streets with the kind of pre-existing heritage as this town has, it invariably clashes and invites derision. Unfortunately such derision is not only directed at the architects and local councillors who approved it, but the town as well. Part of the problem is that proposed development plans can be presented in enticingly attractive ways, from drawing board to press release, much as a newly designed car can. But unless they are built sympathetically, with high-quality, durable and proven materials, however stylish they may appear on paper, their looks often wane as they take on the dubious attributes of a rusty old van. Instead of harmonising within the classic scene Regency Cheltenham grew up with, many new-builds have taken on the guise of cuckoo-in-the-nest impostors that stubbornly refuse to leave.

Acknowledging the genuine interest many people now have for local history and the modern built environment, things have gradually improved and I believe that in the twenty-first century we have a greater say in such matters. In addition to the traditional press notices of old we have additional online access points, such as the 'Planning Portal' and 'Civic Voice' to express our views, especially in relation to controversial planning matters – and we should not shy away from doing so if historic streets and buildings are threatened by some of the ready-mix, flat-pack 'scar-chitecture' thrown up previously, some of which we still have to endure. Such comments can be challenged of course, and need supporting with evidence – like that of the innovative Google Street View Awards made after the public chose the three most beautiful streets in Britain: the Shambles in York, Royal Crescent in Bath and Gray Street in Newcastle – there being nothing remotely modern about them. To me at least, it confirms that many of us ('most people' as the advertisers like to say) prefer acceptably proven styles of architecture and until 'Street Awards' are heaped on diabolical structures such as the 'Millennium Restaurant' (since demolished) or what leaps out from pages 77–8, designers, developers and planners would enjoy greater credibility by paying a little more than lip-service to majority public opinion.

Cheltenham recently picked up a prestigious award for its Promenade. The Google Street Awards category 'Most Picturesque Street' requires entrants be: 'uniquely British and visually charming . . . vibrant, full of character, diverse, walker-friendly and architecturally interesting.' Existing carbuncles on our ancient High Street may preclude such an award but we need search no further for a best-practice template. Whenever we have the opportunity to influence future developments in our still beautiful town, the Google one will suffice!

In conclusion, though not born in Cheltenham, coming from a farming background in the Cotswold village of Naunton, I consider myself fortunate to have arrived here later. Local roots undoubtedly gave me an affinity for the Cotswolds and an appreciation of how the former agrarian 'village' of Cheltenham developed its uniquely stylish and pretentious ways. Enjoying a relatively protected existence in the vale, after discovering efficacious subterranean aquifers, a few eighteenth-century visionaries successfully commercialised its fruits of the earth to the point where royal approval was bestowed on the town in 1788. Five fortuitous weeks of sycophantic activity generated the impetus that propelled a parochial old market town into one of the country's most illustrious promenaded spa towns, sucking in gentry and aristocracy from various parts of this island and its empire. In earlier times, 'the one long street, with small purling Silver Stream or Rivulet' formed the backbone of the embryonic town. Together with its lovely church it outlasted everything and everyone subsequently coming here. This small publication acknowledges these humble beginnings by focusing primarily on this ancient through-route, in recognition of the fact that for centuries it was Cheltenham's only street, well before the addition of the more modern (post-1820) Promenade, pump houses, ample pomp and effete affectations. We will enter as thousands of people have before us, from the 'Top of the Town' – the London end, on the road of that name, before passing through 'Cheltenham Street' and taking occasional peeps elsewhere.

It has been a privilege to follow in the footsteps of the Victorian, Edwardian and later photographers and retaking a few of their shots. In my amateur view, modern photographs can be less inspiring, not only because of the loss of historic buildings and attractive shop fronts but also the clutter of modern street furniture and other equally boring technical differences.[5]

David Hanks, August 2010

---

5. Optical differences between the focal length of modern and nineteenth-century lenses create shifts in perspective, as do differences in lens height above the ground – even when standing in the place where (you think) the original photograph was taken.

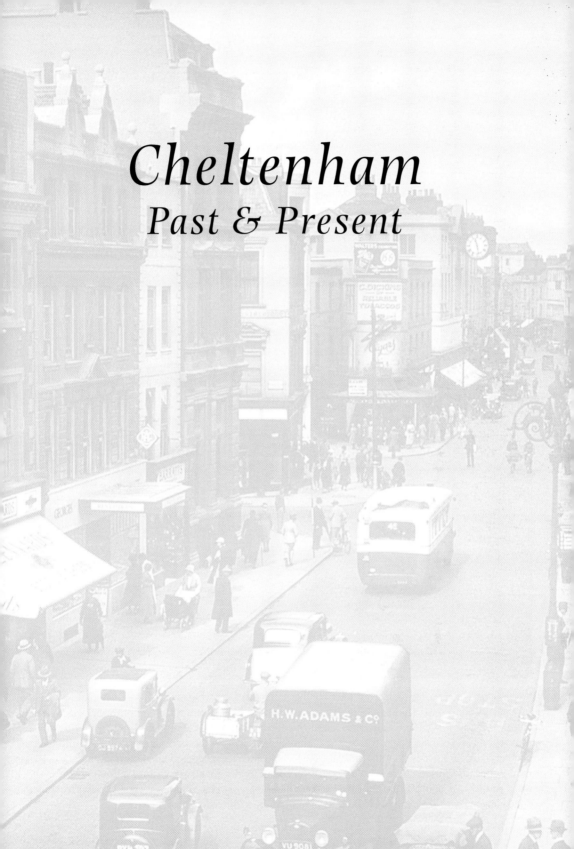

Cheltenham
Past & Present

Following George Rowe's popular (*c.* 1840) lithograph of Cheltenham from Leckhampton Hill, this carte de visite (from about the 1860s) may be the earliest photograph from a similar viewpoint, revealing a long-lost network of quarrying and other local routes, already going back a century or two. It is not known exactly when the earliest quarrying took place on Leckhampton Hill, but it was greatly revived from 1793 onwards for the building of Regency Cheltenham, using stone from this quarry and those at Whittington and Cleeve Hill. The significance of such a tiny photograph is only eclipsed by the impressive time span during which all this hewing and hauling was carried on here, before the plate track railway, lime kilns and quarry workings closed in 1927.

It is practically impossible to take a similar photograph today from where the Victorian photographer placed his camera and tripod. There are a couple of reasons for this. After the early photograph was taken the quarry face was worked further into the hillside for about another sixty years, losing more prehistoric hilltop features and viewpoints. Today's tree-lined escarpment also obscures the same perspective of the town, forcing photographers to stand west of the old cliff-edge to look down Leckhampton Road. Although many old fields were lost under nineteenth- and twentieth-century housing developments, visual continuity exists in other ways, not least of which is the line followed by today's more developed housing corridors of Leckhampton Road (diagonally to the left) and Old Bath Road (diagonally to the right).

The Devil's Chimney, *c.* 1880. An 1830s description of the area reads: 'many curious fragments of rock present themselves to the notice of the traveller, as he ascends the acclivity of which the most striking is that called "the Devil's Chimney". On the precipices may be distinctly traced the remains of a deep entrenchment, by which together with an impregnable fortress, the Romans secured this important station.' The earliest known written record of the Devil's Chimney is Ruff's *Beauties of Cheltenham* guide of 1803, and this quarryman's folly probably dates from after the quarry reopened in 1793. The Roman fort referred to in the 1830s is unlikely; a British Iron Age encampment being more probable, though more of the hewn escarpment was lost between then and the 1920s. Today it is difficult to retake the photograph looking west due to later quarrying and tree growth.

This symbolic landmark enjoys statutory protection as it continues to play a part in the psyche and history of Cheltenham, acquiring almost mystical status. In the author's view it stands as silent sentinel to numerous unknown men who extracted countless thousands of tons of limestone from the Cotswold escarpment over the centuries. Aided largely by gravity and the first known goods railway in the country, by 1810 their industrious hewing and hauling was providing blocks of dressed stone at 1*s* 6*d* per ton (including delivery by tramway) which skilful masons and builders incorporated into Cheltenham's Regency buildings, still at the core of the modern town today.

London Road and Holy Apostles Church (built 1866–71), *c.* 1905. In 1738 the first stagecoach or 'flying machine' from Cheltenham to London advertised to accomplish the journey, if God permitted, in the short space of three days. By the 1730s the 'Old Hereford' coach completed the journey in 26 hours. By 1783 it was reduced to 18 hours and by 1826 a more direct coach route took 10½ hrs. In 1825 engineer Thomas Telford built the New London Road (from here to Six Ways) bypassing Cudnall Street on Cirencester Road. In 1913 a cyclist was killed here in a collision with a tramcar. Until 1974 the junction marked the boundary between the borough and Charlton Kings.

Today, in favourable traffic conditions, a coach from Cheltenham to London takes 2½hrs. Holy Apostles Church is still in use but the adjacent Holy Apostles Junior School relocated in 1967, becoming an antique centre and now a funeral home. The 1870s 'Temperance Society' drinking fountain reminds us of the once-free drinking water in Cheltenham. Compare that with the mountain of plastic bottles we produce today and you realise the Victorians showed us the way forward. We could reduce waste and freely refill plastic bottles many times over from fountains like this.

London Road looking towards the town, with a left turn to the ancient (Domesday) Sandford Mill, 1920s. London Road was the first of Cheltenham's approach roads to be realigned. In 1785 the authorising Act of Parliament said mineral waters had made Cheltenham 'a place of great resort' and would be even better patronised if its roads were improved! This tied in nicely with the opening of the new High Street Assembly Rooms. A couple of local dignitaries, no doubt having suffered sore backsides, drove the improvements through, realigning the detour that had previously seen this old coach route meander into Cheltenham via Kilkenny and Dowdeswell.

Fuller and Maylem's nursery gardens occupied land on the left, abutting the River Chelt, Sandford Mill and Cox's Meadow, until sold for private housing in the 1960s. This shot from March 2010 shows a new eco-friendly house being built on the right. Before 1923 people were unaware that this 94-mile route to London would be part of the 256-mile A40 trunk road from London to Fishguard.

Above: London Road seen in the early 1900s. It was turnpiked here in 1756 and the junction once took its name from the 'Gallows Oak' on the corner. Hales Road (once Gallows Lane or Hangman's Lane, going back to at least 1272) is on the left, while Old Bath Road is on the right. This block of fifteen residential properties, called Oxford Place, was begun in 1819 and partially completed by 1834. The one seen on the corner was later demolished for the widening of Old Bath Road and the extension to the right (below) is modern.

Below: Past phrases like 'freedom of the road' were coined by motorists enjoying easier runs on pre-motorway routes, including this one from London to Wales. Cars like the 1922 Austin Seven added a new dimension: 'Motoring for the Million', with garages like the one seen on page 31. Things could only get worse with regular snarl-ups and in 1960 one formed an 18-mile traffic-jam between here and Oxford.

Upper High Street, near Hales and Old Bath Roads, early 1900s. Batten's Supply Stores, grocers, wine merchant and post office on the left (which opened in 1837), a newsagent, boot repairer, fruiterer, hairdresser, butcher, draper, the Glos Dairy Co., an ironmonger, hardware shop, and on the corner of Hales Road, a chemist (no. 1 High Street) – collectively made this a fairly self-sufficient area.

By 2010 newer heating systems have made many Victorian chimneys redundant. Today this is addressed as London Road, with a café, domestic appliance shop, Keynsham Stores, a betting shop, a Chinese takeaway, a stringed instruments shop and a wood flooring supplier. One or two of the earlier premises on the corner of Hales Road have since been demolished (to the right of the tram in the picture above) – where the town's easterly turnpike was in earlier times.

London Road (Upper High Street) between Hewlett Road and Hales Road, early 1900s. Pedestrian activity and almost everything else moved at a gentler pace with only occasional trams and carriages to watch out for, and with little more than horse droppings deposited on the streets.

Ron Coltman MBE (80), seen here with his bicycle, has never owned a car. He has always walked or cycled to work as a builder and plumber since he was fourteen, including journeys to Gloucester, Coombe Hill, Leckhampton Hill, Cleeve Hill and all over the town. He may well have clocked up as many miles as Mr Austin, who walked the equivalent of nine times round the world on Cheltenham's streets, but his daily perambulations followed a more measurable route (more on that later). Since 1953 Ron has been a great supporter of Sandford Park Lido and his long-term voluntary work there was recognised in 2008.

Above: After ten years of horse-drawn buses, by 1899 the electric tramway revolution rolled into town when the American tramway expert, Thomas Nevins arrived. His expertise saw the Cheltenham & District Light Railway Company formed and the first line between Lansdown and Cleeve Hill via the town centre opened in 1901. This 1905 photograph shows a double track section being laid (by Acme Flooring & Paving Company, Gainsborough) in Upper High Street. It was part of the new line to Charlton Kings via London Road, Holy Apostles, Six Ways, Copt Elm Road and Cirencester Road (New Inn) and back to the town centre. This end of the High Street was also once known as 'the top of the town' and the street's first numbering scheme was introduced in about 1800.

Below: The taller three buildings on the left (32 to 36 High Street) were known as Southampton Place. Beyond this is the entrance to Sandford Park, which was opened in 1928. Berkeley Street joins from the right.

Belle Vue House was originally one of the few detached houses here in 1800 when Cheltenham consisted of little more than High Street. It is seen here in the early 1900s. After the Belle Vue Hotel it became the Irving Hotel, owned by Sir Charles Irving, Conservative MP for Cheltenham between 1974 and 1992. Cheltenham was unrepresented in Parliament until the passing of the Reform Act in 1832.

The busy Upper High Street is now part of the inner ring road as one-way traffic approaches town, past newer private apartments in Irving Court. The vast number of notable folk to have entered Cheltenham along this road would fill volumes, so just one gets a mention here. In 1863 the Revd Charles Lutwidge Dodgson, mathematician, logician, photographer and author (under the familiar name of Lewis Carroll), stayed at the Belle Vue Hotel while visiting the family of his friend Henry Liddell in Charlton Kings. Liddell's daughter Alice is said to have been the inspiration for his heroine in *Alice in Wonderland*.

A scene from the early 1900s, with alfresco meat displayed on the left. This butcher would certainly have known about 'Royal Cheltenham Sausages' even if he didn't sell them. The Bath Road entrance is past the butcher and Norton's Garage on the far corner became one of the earliest (first generation) branches of Tesco in the 1970s. Grosvenor Street is on the right.

'Cotswold Kebabs' sounds incongruous compared with the famous Victorian 'Royal Cheltenham Sausages' but the nation's eating habits have changed considerably during the past century and while it is no longer permissible to display meat in the street, plenty now opt to eat there!

Above: An early 1900s view of the High Street with the Bath Road junction on the left. No. 74 High Street is A.R. Caudle – hats, hosiery and tailoring. No. 73 to the right was a stationers and post office. High Street renumbering occurred in 1820 and again in 1954, allowing alternating north and south side numbers. In 1800 a post office opened at 127 High Street and Sally Saunders ('Old Sall') often took five or six days to deliver letters, saying 'she had something better to do than take a single letter to the bottom of the High Street'!

Below: By 2009 one-way traffic enters Bath Road where pedestrianisation of the High Street commences. This part of High Street (between Belle Vue and Rodney Road) was renamed 'The Strand' in the 1920s at the request of shopkeepers, after a new lighting scheme was introduced. The intention, no doubt, was to evoke the smart London Strand, itself of similar river-bank origins. The shops along Cheltenham's ancient street continue to host a rotating selection of businesses, with newer ground-floor frontages tacked onto older buildings, many at least 200 years old.

Looking east, towards London Road, a poor quality 1900s postcard on which tradesmen appear as rickety as their handcarts. Bath Road is to the right and Grosvenor Street is to the left. Further left is the Restoration Inn which Brewers Ind Coope made a failed application to demolish in 1977. Beyond that the Coopers Arms, rebuilt after it burned down in the early 1900s (both have been here since at least 1839) and beyond them both, the Swan Inn – established in 1725.

The same three pubs trade on the left (north) side of the street. Some businesses remain small local enterprises as others expand and prosper. No. 68 (now the Cutting Room) was Cult Clothing's first shop (in about 1986) after starting out on a market stall in Regent Arcade. Today they are a chain with a £30-40m annual turnover.

Bath Road with Bath Parade on the right, early 1900s. On the left is the entrance to the Salvation Army Citadel (built in 1902), several small shops, Stroud Brewery's Wellington Bar, Strettons Garage and Nortons Garage. Strettons' 'Million Motor Works' was established in 1890 and from 1903 sold and repaired motor bikes and cars, closing in 1912. It became the location of Wicliffe Motors after they left the High Street.

A reminder that modern buildings are not always the direct successors of those in old photographs. In this case several have come and gone, including Wicliffe Motors, House of Holland and, since 1991, Nelson Thornes Publishers in the new building. On the right Cambray Pavilion was razed in 1929, eventually becoming Ebdons Garage. It is now the Moon Under Water pub. The buildings on the right were situated on today's car park. The River Chelt, which runs under the car park and Bath Road, emerges by the old bridge pier and entrance to a newer (1989) Salvation Army Citadel. Of things underground, in 1818, while digging a hole near the Bath Road turnpike, labourers found a perfectly preserved jar with some 1,000 Roman copper and silver coins in it. Like the High Street, this is another ancient way, trodden by millions of folk before we used its comparatively modern tarmacked surface.

A priory of Benedictine monks was founded in about 790 and their building stood somewhere on the left between here and Rodney Road. If that doesn't convince you of the street's antiquity, in 1816 two Roman urns filled with ashes and many coins were found as a High Street drain was laid. The urn was concealed here several centuries before any monks from Cirencester arrived. This photograph from about 1910 is far too modern to hint at anything other than the line of that early street, all else lost in the mists of time, tumult and periodic rebuilding.

When it was part of the A40, the Strand was too narrow for two-way lorry traffic and westbound lorries were diverted through Bath Road, Bath Street and Cambray Place to the High Street. Many upper storeys hark back a couple of centuries, roof lines enjoying a constancy denied to shop fronts which change almost as regularly as ownership. The inappropriate blocks laid here are definitely not Roman, despite their resemblance to some ancient plough-damaged mosaic.

The Leckhampton tram route opened in 1905 and this (bright red and cream) car was photographed entering Cambray Place towards Bath Road and onwards to the foot of Leckhampton Hill. This was the point at which the Leckhampton and Charlton Kings lines diverged.

There has been an almost complete makeover on the north (right) side of the street, with HMV under the concrete overhang. The pedestrianised Strand, Cambray Place and High Street is a safer shopping environment. Bradford & Bingley changed identity to Santander soon after this 2010 photo.

Above: Cambray Place with Cambray House in the distance, early 1900s. Trams passed through Cambray to and from Leckhampton. A barber shop and Mr G. Baldwin, jeweller, watchmaker and optician, are on the right. The 'Corner of Cambray' handcart appears to be another local enterprise.

Below: The left corner reflects the recent takeover of Bradford & Bingley by Santander. Businesses on the right include a tanning shop, a coffee shop, a shoe shop and and branch of Natwest bank.

Above: High Street in 1897 (Cambray Place on the right) decorated for the Prince of Wales' visit. Geeves Wholesale Tea Blenders and Packers are on Cambray corner, which became the Clock Café after 1948. The building was later remodelled with the attractive stone and red brick façade seen today.

Below: The comparative plainness of modern frontages is apparent. Whether this is to deter anti-social behaviour in shop doorways, is more functional, or simply a cost-benefit versus aesthetic-benefit owner's choice, they are less interesting than earlier styles.

The old adage, 'a picture is worth a thousand words', permits a few less as we lament the loss of this beautiful bow-fronted shop window. The several Cheltenham Cadena Cafés enjoyed almost cult status before the last one closed in 1971. People have fond memories of them, whether here (124 High Street) or on the other side (163 High Street) or on the corner of Henrietta Street (260 High Street) or the best-known Cheltenham Cadena (108–10 Promenade) – all established after 1923.

'Together we are Santander' say the commercials, emphasising how quickly things have fallen apart in the banking world. Pointless asking whether the café window is more attractive than the bank, its stark frontage hosting another Spanish-owned, former British bank (as with Bradford and Bingley further east or Alliance & Leicester further west), as bastions of British banking and retailing suffer cross-border take-overs or government bail-outs in the recession. But the business is operating and the staff are employed! Contrast this with the papered-over premises to the left (122 High Street, ex-Woolwich building society) where a notice currently suggests an 'Adult Gaming Centre' for this prime slot. We can but hope this does not become a twenty-first-century High Street casino-banking enterprise.

The Royal Hotel, seen here in about 1950, was in existence since at least 1818. Like the Plough it had a large rear yard with livery stables, the Royal's reaching back to Albion Street. Just before Winchcombe Street is an attractive building in the classical style with columns and pediment. When demolished in 1964 it was Martins Bank, which then occupied the building replacing it. Marks & Spencer were in the arcade/bazaar to the right from the early 1900s. The 1964/5 widening of Winchcombe Street saw the loss of F.E. Higgins, hatters (later Dunn & Co.) on the corner. The new corner building (155 High Street) now houses the town's Cheltenham & Gloucester building society.

The Royal Hotel site became Woolworths in 1957, then a Co-op department store and bank, after which it was redeveloped into the Beechwood Shopping Centre. Opening in 1991, its frontage occupies the full (ten bays) width of the former Royal Hotel, with 127,000sq ft of shops and 400 parking spaces. We can but wonder why this historic site was not called 'The Royal Shopping Centre'.

Lloyds Bank, the Royal Hotel and a busy High Street, 1905. Tramcar no. 13's trial run via Cambray Place at 10.30, returning within thirty minutes, had been to the Leckhampton terminus (top of Leckhampton Road) and Charlton Kings at 11.24 (New Inn terminus) trundling back to Cambray at 11.44. We have absolutely no idea who the two men pushing the handcart are.

Lloyds Bank (now Lloyds TSB) is the main point of continuity, while the former Royal Hotel is now the Beechwood Shopping Centre. On this winter's day postlady Shirley talks to retired colleague Barry Curl as the High Street welcomes shoppers on the final pre-Christmas Saturday in 2009.

The vibrant Assembly Rooms (from an 1860s carte de visite) before Lloyds Bank, with the New Club upstairs since 1816. The Assembly Rooms were here in 1734 and later remodelled. The Plough Hotel is further along, its frontage in line with the lens axis. By the 1830s over 40 horse passenger coaches were arriving here daily with numerous High Street hotels to meet the demand. Cheltenham witnessed the passing of many other types of horse-drawn transport than are seen in one photograph, including lumbering fly-wagons, muck-carts, water-carts, chaises, stagecoaches, horse-buses, ambulances, goods vans, fire engines, hearses, numerous models of private carriages and the fly – the boy racers of their day. After the 'iron horse' arrived in 1840, the High Street saw the demise of the hotels, the introduction of motor vehicles (from the 1890s onwards) and electric trams (1900–30). Until 1876 cattle pens and ancient markets were erected here. Unfortunately they were not captured in this early photograph, as in Gloucester. Cheltenham's last (1811) stagecoach using this street was sold for a fistful of dollars in 1960 by an opportunist local businessman to an equally keen American buyer.

The top view (from the Royal Hotel) was retaken from Optical Express who have enabled a few of us to obtain better views of High Street! The spire of St Mary's Parish Church can be seen above the Regent Arcade.

High Street with the County Co-Operative Drug Company, Imperial Coffee Tavern and Plough Hotel on the left, *c.* 1880. Winchcombe Street (which went under the eighteenth-century name of Bell Lane) is on the right with the eponymous Bell Hotel nearby. There are still no motor cars and this is one of the last High Street photographs before the first cars (about 1896), and the town's first car-related fatality in 1900. In 1859 the GPO began installing letterboxes and on the right is a hexagonal 'Penfold' model (used from 1866 onwards). The Penfold became the standard Post Office design in 1879, leaving Cheltenham with more than any town outside London. Gas lamps like these lit the High Street erratically from 1818 onwards.

The arrival of the motor car saw several High Street garages banking on old business. In this view from the 1910s, Steels Garage (Wolsey & Rover) have moved into the former County of Gloucester Bank after it became Lloyds Bank in 1898 and then moved across the road in 1901. They have cleverly changed the old 'County of Gloucester Bank' signage on the wall to 'County of Gloucester Garage'. In 1910 the Bell Hotel was replaced by the classically styled building, the United Counties Bank. By 1940 this was Martins Bank and by 1970 Barclays. The building was later rebuilt for the Cheltenham & Gloucester building society from Clarence Street. A butcher (Imperial Meat Supply) at no. 103 quite happily displays meats in the open, long before modern health regulations forbade this ancient practice.

Opposite, bottom: The revolutionary impact of mechanical transport on this historic street is a matter of record, but its impact during the twentieth century and beyond may be as nothing compared with the open-ended information technology revolution. The 9 per cent of shopping done on the internet today is forecast to be more than 20 per cent in the next ten years alone, and beyond that we reap what we sow now. In this markedly different cyber-world we are no longer limited to what we see in real shop windows as we browse virtual ones at home. A recent survey showed the average cost of ten goods from the 'High Street' totalling £2,252 compared with £1,785 as the best prices for the same products online, and that 95 per cent of all prices could be beaten online. Cheltenham High Street has bounced back from many challenging moments on its lengthy timeline, as reflected by just one item in the local press (*Cheltenham Examiner*, May 1841) headed, 'Dreadful Scarcity of Money' – 'the most inclement Season which is just past has rendered the Labouring Classes unable to procure the necessaries of life and has pressed with almost equal severity upon the Trading Classes also, and the sacrifice which they have consequently been obliged to make for Ready Money have thrown into the way of those who could afford it, bargains almost incredible . . .' Predicting whether today's recessional belt-tightening, reduced margins, frozen incomes and so-say bargains will sustain our High Street in the long term is difficult. All we dare assume is that future press items will eventually reveal the true cost of it all.

Above: Lloyds (TSB) could hardly foresee it would become the most enduring building on this part of the street as neighbouring hotels (the Lamb, Bell, Crown and Imperial) succumbed to declining trade, shops and arcades. Transport flowed in both directions between London Road and Tewkesbury Road from the earliest times until the mid-twentieth century.

Below: A relatively traffic-free environment may be better for shops and shoppers, so long as enough of us are willing and able to walk from car parks and bus stops. Changing retail habits are forcing the street to keep up and technology may eventually outrun the High Street. We also have some eighteen supermarkets within a 2-mile radius of the town centre, many offering home delivery. Online shopping will continue to impact on the future viability of town centre businesses. Some have already gone and many have adopted a dual-trading approach, online and on-street.

Above: Lloyds Bank built in the neo-Baroque style using Bath stone in 1900 is a good example of twentieth-century continuity. The Royal Hotel (acquired by Woolworths in 1957) is on the right edge of this 1900s view. The gable end of 101 High Street reads, 'Noted House for the Choicest Teas and Coffees', following on from the first recorded coffee house in Cheltenham in 1749. The small building between the hotel and the coffee house at the entrance to Liverpool Place (and Vaults) was 98 High Street, known as Engells Office in the nineteenth century (also see front cover). Here it is occupied by a surgeon dentist; dispensing and photographic chemist, having been a chemists for at least half a century by the early 1900s. The recessed frontage still reflects the front garden of the long gone Vittoria Hotel (early 1800s) vestiges of which are reflected in the same deeper pavement here today.

Below: Traffic still enters this part of the High Street from Rodney Road, leaving via Winchcombe Street, with pedestrian-only stretches east and west, creating a safer, more pleasant shopping environment.

An 1890s view of the High Street with an 1843 advertisement below. As was their wont, Victorian photographers occasionally touched-up glass plate negatives to improve contrast and definition, and insert or remove objects. That said, this is the first proper view of the fourteen-bay Victorian Plough Hotel with shop-filled frontage; (the Introduction has earlier versions). We see it here during the final years of the more genteel equestrian dominated town, something 'Cheltenham Street' had grown familiar with over many centuries. The Plough had a massive rear yard with ample mews for carriages, stabling and smithing; as well as an earlier town hall.

THE PLOUGH YARD & MEWS

Posting at one Shilling and three pence per mile.

THE MEWS

Having been recently re-built, contains Loose Boxes, Large Stall, Harness Rooms,
with every comfort and accommodation for Horses at Livery or Baiting. An extensive covered ride
for exercising in bad weather and good apartments for Grooms and Coachmen.

Excellent Lock-up Coach Houses at Two Shillings per week, and particular attention paid to
Airing of Carriages.

Pleasure and Wedding Parties may be accommodated with Carriages of various descriptions
with grey or bay horses.

Job Horses

By the day, week, month or year. Families requiring the Postillions to wear any particular
livery may be accommodated.

One Horse Flys Always Ready – No fees in town to the Drivers

Hearse and Mourning Coaches with Black Horses, Plumes &c.
And every other Requisite for a Funeral.
Coaches and Omnibuses to all the Stations.

The Plough Hotel (*c.* 1950) with canopied entrance and Winchcombe Street opposite. The Plough was the town's main coaching inn from at least 1727 and a hotel since 1781. The hotel with its lengthy stable yard was replaced by the £23m Regent Arcade development between 1982 and 1984. Dunn & Co, hat makers, occupied the small building on the right edge – demolished when Winchcombe Street was widened in the 1960s.

Having experienced most types of horse-drawn and mechanical transport, sections of the street are currently in a state of flux, accommodating a mix of pedestrians and traffic. Between Winchcombe Street and Pittville Street, the High Street reverts to pedestrian-only (spiced-up by weaving cyclists) and this trend is likely to continue. With Regent Arcade on the left, the road sweeps right into the widened Winchcombe Street. The upper floors and corner wall with the quoins and 'Winchcomb Street' sign on the wall of Thomas Cook (Lloyd & King in early picture) have survived. Thomas Cook was in the Promenade from 1903, relocating to this corner of Winchcombe Street in 1995.

High Street, *c*. 1945. On the left is Peacocks and then H.E. Steels Garage, with 'County Of Gloucester Garage' on its upper wall. I believe this was the former 'County of Gloucester Bank', the name being adapted after cars arrived on the scene. It started as Pitt's Bank; Joseph Pitt (of Pittville fame) and his partner John Gardner (of the brewery) formed the new bank. When the financial panic of 1825 threatened a run on the bank, Gardner made a risky journey to London and back in record time, bringing back enough money to pay shareholders and save the bank.

Cheltenham & Gloucester building society occupies 155 High Street at the corner of Winchcombe Street to the left of Next. Chelsea Building Society (this side of Beechwood) has recently been taken over by Yorkshire Building Society, leading to more local job losses. Smart car drivers like this can still drive from Rodney Road to Winchcombe Street, but for how much longer is anyone's guess.

The High Street towards Boots Corner shortly before electric trams arrived, *c.* 1900. The Lamb and George hotels are open for business and numerous awnings on the north side of the street protect shop displays from sunlight, common before the invention of UV-resistant glazing. Blinds are still used today by some retailers with a local manufacturer in town. Numerous people captured in these single moments of elapsing time were totally unaware that a century on others might be slightly curious as to who they were and what they were doing that fine day in their Victorian High Street.

In the winter of 2009/10 the customary pedestrian bustle fills a traffic-free section of the High Street; people mostly unaware that a century on others will be similarly curious about them. Marks & Spencer's modern clock has become the High Street's modern timepiece.

Above: A 1900 view of Winchcombe Street (spelt without the final 'e' until about 1930). Mr Kilbey at 20 Winchcombe Street (with spectacles above window) was 'watchmaker, jeweller and optician'. The street was widened between 1962 and 1964 and all the shops on the right were cleared away.

Below: The wider street is one-way and Winchcombe House runs from the C&G to Albion Street. The MEB electricity showroom previously on the right is now a branch of Ladbrokes and the left side remains fairly intact. The large white building on the right (beyond Albion Street) was the Gaumont Cinema after 1932 where the Beatles performed in 1963, Cliff Richard in 1964 and the Rolling Stones in 1965, ending its life as the Odeon Cinema and with a planning application submitted to turn it into a large nightclub. Highbury Congregational Church stood on the site before 1932.

This view from about 1915 includes (left) John Williams & Co. Coal Merchants, Vanderplank (fashions and furs) and the Singer Sewing Machine Company. On the right are the Palace Picture Theatre, Blue Taxi Cabs (with taxi outside), the Lamb Hotel and Alfred Miles 'Motor Works Garage No. 3' occupying the former George Hotel site. The Palace Picture Theatre opened as such in 1910 and closed in 1954, but animated films were shown here from 1863.

After 1935 things changed on the right, sweeping away hotels, garages and theatres. It is now a case of looking above ground level to spot any visual continuity, and the previous three-storey height of the former George and Lamb hotels was not required by modern Marks & Spencer after they moved from The Arcade, further east.

In this 1930s view we see Timothy Whites chemists and household goods at 148–50 High Street, which became Timothy Whites & Taylors in 1935. The chemist side of the business was taken over by Boots in 1968. As I write, a 1920s Timothy Whites (Cheltenham) poison bottle sells on Ebay for £21.97, again proving the power of nostalgia – Ebay sourcing quite a few old pictures in this book.

Shoppers on the final (2009) Saturday before Christmas, part-way through a recession, with O2 mobile phone shop (right) and Vodafone beyond Burger King (left), two of seven mobile phone shops, with none before the 1990s. These shops further demonstrate how historic streets have to constantly adapt within our ever changing technological world.

No. 384 High Street on the left, was Simmons, watchmaker & jeweller, next to Cheltenham Operatic & Dramatic Society, 1900s. Regent Street is the next turning left and Pittville Street is on the right behind the nearest tram. Alfred Miles Motor Garage has now replaced the Lamb Hotel on the right.

On a cold winter's day in 2009 sunshine over-exposes the front of Marks & Spencer (once the George and Lamb hotels). The street is traffic-free and these days chewing gum is more costly to remove than horse dung, the latter being useful elsewhere! Another phone shop is on the left (phones 4u) as this line of business thrives with its 'must-have' range of products we all somehow once managed without.

Boots signage proclaims: 'The Largest Retail Chemists to the World', but they do not yet occupy the corner of North Street in this photograph from the early 1900s. Prior to Boots acquiring the site it was the National Provincial Union Bank of England and the Wilts and Dorset Bank, and in fact a bank strongroom remains in Boots' basement today. Boots façade is still without the Classical columns and pediment that came later.

Part way through an election campaign (April 2010) we are heading towards Republic (the store on the left). The shops on the opposite side, between Boots and Pittville Street, were built during one of the familiar 1960s redevelopment phases, leaving the more enduring Boots as the older relation here today.

Above: A 1930s view of the A40 towards the Midland Bank shows five shops, later demolished to accommodate three new ones, arguably no less acceptable than earlier Victorian pseudo-Classical designs displacing earlier medieval or Elizabethan buildings. Today more people seem to appreciate the older styles than some of the stark Modernism of our own times. Baily Jones & Co. (drapers) are on the right. The inset picture shows the A40 sign by the roundabout, towards Gloucester via the Promenade, *c.* 1960.

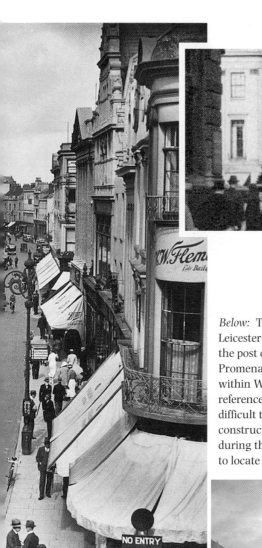

Below: This two-storey concrete block houses the Alliance & Leicester (now part of the Santander group), WHSmith and the post office (from 1874 to 1987 the post office was in the Promenade, from 1987 to 2008 at 225–7 High Street and now within WHSmith), and Carphone Warehouse. Without historic reference points such as the corner bank it is increasingly difficult to place earlier views among the less elegant 1960s constructs. The Baily Jones corner, opposite, was removed during the widening of Pittville Street (it has not been possible to locate any early photographs of the narrower Pittville Street).

We are now at the centre of Edwardian Cheltenham where the line of this ancient street forges ahead to Tewkesbury Road. The newer (post-1820s) Promenade joins almost unnoticed from the left and North Street from the right (originally Greyhound Lane after the Greyhound Inn which stood on the corner). North Street's name has been in use since at least 1763. This early 1900s view shows the Empress Tea Rooms on its south-west corner.

HSBC is on Promenade corner with no. 1 Clarence Street beyond, the canopied 'Cobbler's Corner' next door (ex-Charles Dickins, tobacconists, at 202 High Street) and Boots on the right, each surviving as more enduring town centre buildings in the twenty-first century.

A 1940s view into Lower High Street at Boots Corner, the Army Recruiting Office (here in the 1920s), Charles Dickins, tobacconist (established 1889) and the town clock is now above 'Woolworths 6d Store'. Wards department store (1901–67) now extends round the corner into North Street. After the removal of the Colonnade building (see p. 66), the traffic island was installed on this busy A40 intersection.

A century ago the building on the corner of North Street was the Empress Tea Rooms, then it became Wards Drapery Store which closed in 1967. The site was redeveloped for Littlewoods in 1973 and later for Primark. The 1955 renumbering addresses it as 201–7 High Street.

Above: A 1900s view of the Colonnade (north end of the Promenade) to the National Bank and Boots in the High Street. Martin & Co. (jeweller & watchmaker) was established in 1806 in the Strand moving to 19 the Promenade (previously Imperial Circus) in 1841. Shirer & Hadden are next door in the 'island block' and eventually occupied most of the new building as Shirer & Lances. Sharpe & Sons on the right made 'Gentlemen's Military Boots' and 'Ladies' Court Boots and Shoes'.

Below: Beyond Martin's less impressive modern clock, the block was rebuilt after 1937. Jones the Bootmaker occupies premises between County Court Road and Cavendish House, the lovely canopied balcony preserved. Bollards now delineate a pedestrianised area of the Promenade between here and Crescent Terrace further south.

Above: The term 'Boots Corner' doesn't apply to these early 1900s views because the building on the corner of North Street was the National Provincial Union Bank. It was however the 'Tram Centre' and later known as 'town centre' after trams ceased running in 1930. Today it is hard to believe that until the mid-twentieth century, traffic on the A40 from London turned left into the Promenade and on to Gloucester and Wales. Traffic from the Gloucester direction came down the Promenade, round the 'island block' into Clarence Street, turning right here towards Oxford, which is straight ahead in this view.

Below: The former Midland Bank (now HSBC) and Boots
are relatively unscathed by twentieth-century High Street
modernisation. With 10,000 vehicles and 20,000 pedestrians
crossing paths here daily, pedestrian priority will eventually
prevail, with only buses and delivery vehicles allowed, with
no apparent rush to create a central pedestrian precinct – first
planned and unveiled in 1970. A 6 a.m. to 10 p.m. traffic census
in 1937 recorded 6,869 cars, 7,408 bicycles and 174 horses
using High Street.

Dodwells Newsagent's 'Demolition Sale' marks the imminent closure of this Victorian building (then 361–2 High Street). It was demolished in 1937, the roundabout installed,leaving the 1920s section of the island block and Shirer & Lances department store behind, the store closing in 1979. The building seen here was at the north end of the Promenade facing the High Street with Clarence Street to the right (where the vehicle is emerging) and the Colonnade/Promenade the far side. The former Midland Bank (HSBC) is visible in the left of both pictures.

Until the A40 was re-routed from the town centre, police officers regularly directed traffic there. An enduring character in this picture is Mr Tom Breen of Cheltenham. Tom joined the Gloucestershire Constabulary in 1938, doing plenty of traffic duty around the town. He was called up in the Second World War and served in the Grenadier Guards Tank Corps. Wounded in action in France soon after the D-Day landings he rejoined the Gloucestershire Constabulary after the war, serving until retirement in 1968. Tom (94) still enjoys trips to the town centre by bus and occasional days out at the races, but had to give up his golf due to reduced mobility.

The Colonnade's first stone was laid in 1791 but it never reached the proposed 2,000ft line of sixty-four elegant houses with covered promenade leading to the developing spa area. Fashions changed and sections were removed between 1849 and 1882 resulting in a wider Promenade entrance beyond this block. Victorian buildings were added at this end and removed in 1937. This 1940s view shows the one-way Colonnade section of A40 into the Promenade. Shirer & Lances department store occupied most of this post-1937 structure built north of Martin & Co., jewellers at the far (southern) end.

Pigeon netting aside, the view from Boots is much the same, minus the roundabout. One-way traffic still flows round the island block but after it was de-trunked, the A40 was re-routed on the south-east side of town, leaving mostly town traffic using the full length of the Promenade.

Boots in 1950, next to John Collier (tailor), Stead & Simpson (footwear), Lilley & Skinner (footwear) and Barnett Hutton (costumiers). The corner building opposite (dating from 1880) was the Worcester City & County Bank and later Midland Bank Ltd. In 1966 the roundabout was removed for a new one-way system (one of several variants; the first was trialled in 1948). In 1974 High Street and Promenade were de-trunked and the A40 re-routed along Old Bath Road, Thirlstaine Road and Lansdown Road.

Since de-trunking the High Street and Promenade, limited pedestrianisation has taken place. Boots is next to Game and Clarks shoe shop. HSBC is opposite and roughly where the Great Stone stood in 1695, almost certainly the base of the even more ancient medieval High Cross (not to be confused with the remains of the Market Cross in the parish churchyard today or the Butter Cross which once stood in the centre of the High Street between Winchcombe Street and the Plough Inn, near a Market House on stone pillars, pulled down in 1796).

Above: North Place (built by 1820) acquired gas lamps soon after the first High Street lamps in 1818. By 1852, 756 gas lamps illuminated the town. When this lamplighter was photographed in about 1905, Mr J.W. Austin had been Cheltenham lamplighter for 44 years. He retired in 1906 and is said to have walked 224,840 miles around the town lighting lamps (equivalent to nine times round the world). It is unlikely Mr Austin's incredible 'feat of endurance' was ever exceeded by anyone else in Cheltenham, but I am happy to be corrected on that.

Below: In April 2010 the far building is a law firm, then the Parrot pub, a three-storey apartment block and the United Services Club; leaving these buildings relatively intact. In 1948 2,000 street lamps illuminated 90 miles of Cheltenham's roads. The one in front of the Parrot is now one of 11,611 electric lamps and 1,936 electric signs and bollards, successors of the first electric lamps installed in High Street in 1897.

A 1900s view towards Boots Corner with The Famous Gents' Outfitters right, established here in 1886. Intersport in St George's Hall at 252 High Street, further west, also belongs to The Famous.

The Famous is on the right with yet another mobile phone shop opposite. The block-surface street gives the appearance of a pedestrian environment but care is needed in this 'shared space' used by one-a-minute buses. In those far-off, less risk-averse times of electric trams, the tram lines at least gave visual warning of their emission-less presence.

Lower High Street in the 1900s between Bennington Street and Henrietta Street. Rees Jones clothing shop is on the left and the Victorian Grammar School is opposite. Front right was the entrance to Cheltenham's fourth (largest) market house, built behind a wide arcade (now Bennington Street entrance) by Lord Sherborne in 1822 to clear the restricted thoroughfare of the old Market House. In 1867 this market moved further west to the old Albion Brewery ground on Gloucester Road, but it was not until 1876 that all cattle pens and fairs were totally removed there from High Street.

In December 2009 the opposing faces of post-1960s Modernism square-up to older styles with a few teeth pulled on the left, where they resist the newer design contagion with mixed results. National and multinational chains now display their trade marks along most of the High Street.

Above: A 1920s view towards the town centre. Georges' (caterers) steam lorry is on the right. On the left at 156 High Street are E. Pobjoy (confectioner) and E.H. Walkley (gramophones and records) with Osborne House beyond (drapers and milliners). The town clock (1827–1958) is over the old Market-house which after 1852 was used by the Magistrates and the Town Commissioners and later the Borough Council who sold it to F.W. Woolworths in 1915 when they moved to the Promenade. Tesco bought it in 1960; a serious fire destroyed it in 1969, it was rebuilt and Tesco Home and Ware moved out in 1983.

Below: The 'Centre Stone' on the corner of Bennington Street (just visible in both pictures) sits at the east end of this 1960s development when all between Henrietta Street and Bennington Street was demolished. Poundland on the left is one of 260 stores nationwide. Here they are about to cross the street to larger vacant premises opposite, with Peacocks filling another empty shop to the right.

Early schooling in Cheltenham is believed to have taken place at St Katherine's Chantry over the north porch in the parish church. In 1574 Richard Pate of Minsterworth (Recorder and Member of Parliament for Gloucester), built the first Free Grammar School on land granted by Elizabeth I on the north side of High Street, where it stood until 1887. The solid-looking Elizabethan school was photographed for this carte de visite from about the 1860s. It is a rare glimpse of Cheltenham's pre-Regency Cotswold stone High Street buildings, more reminiscent of Campden than Cheltenham. It had become too small for its 150 scholars, despite a new schoolroom added to the rear and expanding into Yearsley's Boarding House. Had the Victorians been a little more protective of their heritage, put sentiment aside and gone ahead with their initial plan to build the new school in Christchurch Road (the Ladies' College sports field today), this Elizabethan gem might have survived as one of only three historically un-clad Cotswold stone buildings in Cheltenham at the time, cherished like the parish church is today. This particular act of vandalism that shocked many occurred in 1887.

The new 1887–9 Victorian Grammar School stood here until 1965, succeeded by its first short-lived replacement in Hesters Way (1965–95). The school's former High Street location, together with Osborne House and a variety of shops between Bennington Street and Henrietta Street was razed, leaving the town with this modern concrete curtain which (in the author's view) has the same visual appeal as the back of the passing bus. This occurred in our times, with people showing the same indifference towards the town's Victorian buildings as they did for the *Schola Grammatica* – accepting that they mimicked an earlier style and that the concrete wall outside Wilkinson's does have a Civic Society plaque to Richard Pate – where Sainsbury's store was before relocating on the western outskirts. Cheltenham Original Brewery buildings and the Fleece Hotel were to the left of the grammar school and the school and brewery yards occupied a large area behind the High Street frontage. The brewery complex was replaced by the Brewery Shopping Centre in 2006.

A 1920s selection of interesting frontages. The Elizabethan-styled Victorian Grammar School for boys cost £10,000 with a playing field behind. To its left are Cheltenham Original Ale and Porter Brewery (dating from about the 1820s) and the Fleece Hotel (1700s–1960s) on the corner of Henrietta Street (out of view). The modern grammar school was built in Hesters Way in 1965.

How will future generations react to what was bequeathed them here? Honest descriptions are best left unprinted and such views are understandable. In milder terms, the joined-up concrete between Bennington Street and Henrietta Street reminds us of the brutalistically sterile 1960s school of design many now regard as built illiteracy. Sadly, it is often too late when insensitive redevelopment like this is acknowledged as worse than what it replaced. Not permitted in Cotswold high streets such as Chipping Campden or Chipping Sodbury, so why in Cheltenham we might ask?

Henrietta Street is on the left with the Brewery, Fleece Hotel and Victorian Grammar School beyond, early 1900s. St George's Street is to the right with Whitaker & Co., wine and spirit merchants, Fredrick Wright's cigar warehouse and a constable observing all on his well-trodden beat. Some 250 years of commercial brewing came to an end in 1998 when Flowers Brewery closed and Whitbread announced a £30m leisure development for the site. In reality, in 1600 there were at least 12 maltsters and one cooper in Cheltenham carrying on an age-old tradition of family brewing.

Two constables pause while patrolling, 2009. Behind them is a tanning studio, a fast-food outlet, a tea room and a furniture studio. The edifice on the left (from Henrietta Street to Bennington Street) is owned by NFU Mutual and part of their ten-year plan includes an entranceway through to the new Brewery Shopping Centre from the High Street; any other improvements to it are as yet unknown.

A 1900s view of the Fleece Hotel on the corner of Henrietta Street (formerly Fleece Lane, where the gaol was). Describing itself here as a 'Family and Commercial Hotel' it had deep agrarian roots going back to at least 1783. 'Farmer George' (King George III) didn't choose to stay here in 1788!

In this 2010 view, work on 'Digital Cheltenham' takes place under the street, and the on-your-bike small-island project sits on the surface, which may have appeared more logical on the drawing board!

A 1900s view in Lower High Street with St George's Street on the left and Ambrose Street on the right. Today the corner premises are occupied by Hutchinsons Vision and Hi-Fi. Next door is a Polish sandwich bar, the Joyce Brooks lingerie shop, another sandwich shop and a modern charity shop, replacing James Tinkler's timber-framed (1816) basket, brush and rope shop, another piece of Cheltenham's historic jigsaw sacrificed on the altar of 1960s modernisation.

From here to Gloucester Road and Tewkesbury Road new borough signage calls Lower High Street 'West End'. Whether such rebranding serves to add or detract from this side of the town's long-term commercial viability remains to be seen.

Lower High Street, *c.* 1900. The Kings Head Hotel is in the distance, Matthew Adcock's boot repair shop (established 1879), another Coffee Tavern and a shop selling 'Dog Boxes' are seen here in this less-photographed part of the town. Planned tram lines were never laid in Lower High Street because the company concluded its residents would have been unable to afford regular travel on its cars. Does that stigma live on today? If so, it is based on a false premise and the area has much to offer.

Since then a post office with a public phone came and went and while most people now have a mobile phone, post offices are far less accessible. Adcocks Shoes moved to Bath Road in 1987, run by the fifth generation of the family. Now we have a student let office, a fast-food outlet, a Thai supermarket, and a 'Money shop'. The former Kings Head Hotel is one of just two pubs on the street today.

The Lower High Street in the 1900s with Devonshire Street to the left and the railway bridge and gas works at the end. Many town pubs were closed by magistrates in about 1905, drastically reducing the 300-odd existing previously. In Lower High Street alone (to Gloucester Road) were the Full Moon, Red Lion, Kings Head, George (seen here on corner of Milsom Street), Wheatsheaf, Shakespeare, Roebuck, Golden Heart, Nags Head, Spread Eagle, Sun, White Lion, Harp and Golden Cross, which collectively must have rendered the street the antithesis of the town's more prestigious Promenade.

Today the Lower High Street has two Irish-themed pubs and a variety of small businesses. Less prestigious it may be, without the larger stores and multi-nationals that have seen other streets adopt the cloned-town syndrome, but West End retains much of its earlier identity. In 1996 local residents were consulted about plans to spend £10m on the area! It still struggles for funding and credibility on the part of hesitant shoppers, to aid regeneration and sustain smaller enterprises making it what it is – a part of Cheltenham worth a visit, so come on down. Ron Prewer, seen here with his daughter Jane who works nearby, knows this part of town as well as any local historian.

At the far (west) end of the High Street we arrive at the junction with Gloucester Road, presided over by this fine building. The Cheltenham Gas Light & Coke Company was established 1818 and these are the 1880s Gas Offices. This gathering no doubt included company employees, standing comparatively safely in the road for a photograph from about 1910. The gasometers along Gloucester Road were removed in the 1970s. A century earlier this was the lower turnpike's location and also where the 1809 horse tramway from Gloucester Docks terminated, with coal and other goods for the modern town in operation until 1859. Traces of the tramway still are visible in the from of the extra wide footpath on Gloucester Road (between St George's Road and Queen's Road).

Preserving this building is something Cheltenham can be justly proud of. The former gas works site behind was developed mostly by Tesco as a superstore in the 1990s. Today the old Gas Offices house several small businesses including a call centre and insurance company and some employees were good enough to stand safely on the pavement in March 2010.

Elegant wearers of modern fashion promenade past Cheltenham's premier department store in the 1890s. Cavendish House opened in 1826 at 3 Promenade. It was greatly expanded in 1844 and several times thereafter, acquiring nearby premises and unashamedly aiming its quality merchandise at the town's nobility and aristocracy, who had previously made long and tedious journeys to Cavendish House in London (near Cavendish Square). In 1891 a visitor described the windows as, 'rich massive, hand-carved pillars of solid mahogany, one window with a mass of magnificent carving, whence fall long drooping swags of carved flowers'. By 1938 it boasted 138,000sq ft of floor space. Post-1964 changes saw the old façade and much behind it swept away during an £800,000 modernisation programme. During this work excavations found the remains of passages under Regent Street, a lost road and house. In 1972 it became part of Harrods Provincial Group after which the *Echo* labelled it: 'The Harrods of the West'. It now occupies 32–48 Promenade and is part of the House of Fraser Group.

In 2010 Cavendish House has 390 members of staff and 105,860sq ft of trading footage. The Food Hall closed in 1997.

Above: Before 1818 this was a swampy lane with a plank across the River Chelt. In 1818 it was upgraded into Sherborne Walk with an avenue of trees (similar to Old Well Walk) between High Street and Sherborne Spa (Imperial Spa – later the Queen's Hotel site) with an elegant wrought iron bridge over the Chelt, becoming the Promenade in about 1820. This is a classic 1900s view when Cheltenham was still a fashionable watering hole and where much of the upper class society promenaded. The former Imperial Hotel on the right became the exclusive Imperial Club in 1856 taking its name from the former Imperial Hotel in the same building. The successor of the Imperial Club moved to purpose built premises next to the town hall by 1876, described as, 'open to visitors of approved rank in society'. The Promenade building was the general post office from 1874 to 1987. Today it is Waterstone's bookshop.

Below: This section of the Promenade is now
pedestrianised with lower foliage on younger trees.

The Promenade looking south towards the Queen's Hotel on an 1860s carte de visite. The River Chelt was initially bridged in the rear ground of this photograph, going underground by about 1820. Fine residential terraces were built on both sides and in Victorian times many on the east side were converted into handsome shops. Left of Ormond Place is 9 Promenade Terrace (Sandringham House) and C.W. Norman, glass and china merchant. Right of Ormond Place at no. 10 is Nixon's, also glass and china merchant; two 'Chinamen' trading shoulder-to-shoulder from the 1850s. Gradually the Promenade became a celebrated and exclusive shopping area, its fine houses and classical Literary and Philosophical Institute giving way to more shops. The last privately owned house (no. 21) was in 1982.

R.F. Beard Ltd, jewellers (on the left of Ormond Place) was bought by Waite & Son (established 1804) who relocated to Sandringham House from the High Street in the 1930s. On the right of Ormond Place is 'CC' ladies' fashion shop.

The Promenade, looking north towards the High Street and featuring Woodward's Music Warehouse, 1860s. George Woodward, organist at St Mary's Church and pianoforte teacher, had been trading for half a century when this shot was taken. The Promenade's first electric lighting experiments were carried out in 1889, a year after Cheltenham was first connected by telephone with trunk lines of the Western Counties and South Wales.

Frontages and transportation methods change but the Promenade's ambience is still essentially the same. Many of the chestnut trees planted in 1818 were felled between 1977 and 1980 owing to their poor condition. It is interesting to reflect that had Lord Sherborne's descendant (John Dutton of Sherborne purchased the Manor of Cheltenham outright for £1,200 in 1628) not built Sherborne Spa in 1818, it may not have become the 'Sherborne Walk' that became the 'Promenade' – and all that subsequently flowed along it from High Street.

The Promenade 1920s. Dale Forty Piano Merchants (left of Imperial Lane) were here from the late nineteenth century, with a piano manufactory in Regent Street. The Cadena Café is on the right corner and in 1906 was one of the two 'Oriental Café Company' premises (also at 395 High Street) becoming 'Cadena Cafés Ltd' in 1923. The Promenade Cadena had this attractive canopied roof terrace.

The once-popular roof terrace is empty with modern shops below. Since 2008 two newer businesses are Joules and Vinegar Hill, occupying the former (split) premises of Habitat. The Promenade was voted as having the finest shopping frontage in the country in 2005.

Built in 1874, this 1900s view shows 'The New Club' in the north-west corner of Imperial Gardens. Before 1900 the exclusive 'Gentlemen's Club' had been in the High Street Assembly Rooms. In 1959 plans were drawn up to replace the building with offices; it was demolished in 1976 and the site developed into a modern office block. Whatever happened to those beautiful canopies?

The 'New Club' viewed from Imperial Gardens, *c*. 1950. It was replaced by the Quadrangle in 1977.

The Quadrangle is a boxy glasshouse building that quite simply fails to complement the area. It commenced life as head office for Gulf Oil (GB) Ltd. Gulf moved out in 1993 to another new head office built on the site of 'Rosehill' in New Barn Lane (later occupied by UCCA). Today several businesses partially occupy the Quadrangle.

In 1837 wagon loads of previously dressed stone from the Imperial or Sherborne Spa were carted down the Promenade from their original (1818) location, vacating the site for the new Queen's Hotel. It was rebuilt here on the corner of St George's Road, becoming 'Mr Powell's Rooms' with Imperial Lodge behind (see photograph, left, from an 1860s carte de visite). In the 1892 photo below, the ground is being prepared for the building of the Italian-styled Neptune's Fountain in Portland stone, using water from the River Chelt now in a conduit underneath the Promenade. The former spa building also served as furniture and carpet warehouse, Dale Forty piano warehouse and later as tea rooms. In 1937 it was demolished for the building of the Regal Cinema, then EMI's largest in the country with 1,839 seats (later the ABC) closing in 1981. The ABC was demolished and new offices housing a finance company built in its place. It remains in use as offices today (see lower left photograph).

The Municipal Offices are in the modern photograph below, but it was still private houses in the top photograph. In 1915 the Municipal Office moved here from High Street, occupying the central five houses in 'Harward's buildings', expanding into thirteen of the nineteen houses by 1958.

Looking south in Imperial Gardens people enjoy a concert in front of the Queen's Hotel, 1920s. Today it is hard to understand why Cheltenham removed this band stand in 1948 and sold it to Bognor Regis where it is today (see inset picture). Disposing of such pieces of the 'family silver' in this way has deprived bands from entertaining us in this beautiful Promenade Gardens location. Trees seem to have been thoughtfully omitted in the south-west corner permitting a view of the hotel from the gardens.

In 2008 a fountain with a statue of Gustav Holst was erected on the bandstand's footprint commemorating the composer (born in Cheltenham in 1874). On this 2009 winter's day, only leafless trees enable us to see the hotel from the gardens in which some Cheltenham residents obligingly pose. Back, left to right: Sarah, Mark, Roy, Mark, Martin, Ron, Shirley, Robin, Lucy, Suzanne, Bernard and Anita. Front row parts were less knowingly played by two-year-old Sam, sister Sophie and cousin Freya.

The Queen's Hotel was completed in 1838 on the site of the disassembled Imperial or Sherborne Spa. That was some three years before Mr Palmer's 1841 photographic studio opened north of the hotel in nearby Imperial Nursery. His studio was in a double row of small business units on the site of the yet-to-be-built Winter Gardens (1870–1930s) behind the future town hall (built 1902). This 1860s carte de visite was not produced by Mr Palmer, but is still among the earliest topographical shots taken in the town.

'The Queens', as she is now affectionately known, remains Cheltenham's premier hotel for visitors from all parts of the world and frequently overflows when events such as the Literature Festival and Cheltenham Races are held. Currently under French ownership, an application has been made to remove the conservatory to add a new east wing. This 2007 photograph was taken before the Sebastopol gun plinth was restored (see p 98).

The Queen's Hotel livery yard, stables and carriage block
was a busy place. It is seen here in about 1880. It offered:
'excellent stabling for hunters; open and closed carriages,
wedding equipages, hearses, funeral and mourning carriages'.
Horse-drawn carriages were the only acceptable all-weather
means of conveying visitors and their luggage between hotel,
railway stations and town until gradually replaced by motor
transport in the early twentieth century. The inset picture
shows a newer (solid-tyred) motor bus jointly contracted between The Queen's, Belle Vue, Royal, Plough,
Lamb, Fleece and Carr's Hotels. Imperial Square's new (1998) southern, (faux-Regency) terrace, 'The
Broadwalk', incorporated part of the former stable block between The Queens and Trafalgar Street. The
Queens retained enough of its old stable yard for car parking between the rear of Montpellier Spa Road
and The Broadwalk (left and right respectively in lower picture).

The Winter Garden (1878–1940s) was taken over by the Borough Council in 1895. Seen here in about 1900, it hosted various events ranging from Shakespeare plays, ice-skating, cinema, exhibitions and First World War aircraft assembly. Abutting the rear of the town hall it had to go, due to the exigencies of war and its deteriorating ironwork. The bandstand survived for ten more years and the railings were removed for scrap during the Second World War.

The Imperial Gardens, Winter Gardens (roughly where Mr Palmer's 1841 portrait studio stood), the bandstand, town hall, and New Club. The Queen's Hotel stable yard is in the lower left of the picture, and the Ladies' College is in the upper left.

The view from The Queen's Hotel over Imperial Gardens and Cleeve Hill beyond. If the trees in the centre were removed, the view both ways would be as good as it used to be.

In 1858, following the Siege of Sebastopol during the Crimean War on the Black Sea, two captured bronze cannon were installed on plinths in front of the Queen's Hotel to commemorate the victory. This carte de visite from the 1860s shows proud men and boys who no doubt knew men who had fought there during the siege and its half-dozen battles, including Alma and Inkerman. Large crowds gathered daily for the bulletins posted in the *Cheltenham Examiner* office. They would also have known that soldiers returning from the Crimea brought back the first snowdrops that proliferate in Britain today. They would have known that Florence Nightingale nursed a good few men to the point they were able to return home with snowdrops. The boys would have been too old to fight during the First World War and totally unaware that the cannon would be removed in 1942 for essential Second World War munitions.

The one remaining plinth was tastefully restored by the Borough Council in 2009, another fitting memorial to many local men who gave their lives on foreign soil.

In this rare 1860s carte de visite, the Victorian photographer has recorded a no-nonsense maintenance gang in front of The Queen's Hotel. While it is doubtful they had taken afternoon tea there, their work ensured that those doing so arrived in carriages over roads with a minimum of potholes, something we still crave for today. Whether the road surface was tarmacked or was still sandy at this date is unknown.

Clarence House provides the same attractive backdrop, but the modern five-man repair team (summer 2010) use a paver and double-roller that would have amazed the Victorian team.

The Promenade, looking north from the Queen's Hotel, *c.* 1875. There are no parking restrictions or congestion. The Promenade is some fifty years old with carriage drivers and others pausing for the photographer, maybe hoping to see the result in his studio window a few days later.

135 years later and it is cheaper for modern carriages to drive straight through. Today's parking charges range from £1.60 for an hour to £10 for 10 hours (April 2010). I prefer a bicycle, which is free to park at the moment! The Quadrangle office building (p. 91) is on the right.

Queen's Circus towards the Rotunda, 1880s. The 1843 Royal House (now Hanover House) is on the right. Details of the (since demolished) building on the far left, in the north-west corner of Montpellier Gardens, are speculative. Mr Suter's photographic studio was still at the far side of Royal House at this date.

Hanover House is occupied by Barclays bank, a pizza restaurant and letting agents. The Caryatid figures were modelled on those supporting the roof of the Acropolis temple, the Erechtheion in Athens.

William James Suter's portrait studio was in Royal House, Montpellier, from 1874 and he took this photograph for one of his own cartes de visite, the rear of which (below) describes his versatile services as, 'Artist, Miniature Painter & Photographer . . . enlargements on porcelain, paper or canvas, finished in water colors, oils or crayons' – the Victorian equivalent of a modern digital photographic studio.

In 1905 the southern end of Royal House (since renamed Hanover House) containing Montpellier Coal Exchange and Mr Suter's studio was rebuilt, becoming the National Provincial Bank. The ground floor is now a pizza restaurant, with other businesses in the building. The spire of St Andrew's Presbyterian Church is not visible in the early photograph because it was not built until 1885.

Right: The Old, Royal or King's Well Pump Room, *c.* 1870. The distant building is Royal Well Methodist Chapel (1864–1965) at the north end of the elm tree-lined Old Well Walk in St George's Road and in line with St Mary's Church spire which is behind it. This rare photograph shows the (1849/50) Roman Corinthian style Pump Room designed by Samuel Olney, replacing the Old Well Spa in 1848 (no photographs of this exist). It also served as a theatre, assembly hall and music hall, with spa waters served from a small conservatory at one end. It became too small for these functions and coupled with the decline in use of the waters, it fell obsolete. In 1889 it was purchased by the Governors of the Ladies' College as the college expanded towards its north side. It was repaired and used by the college until 1897 when it was replaced by the present Princess Hall. The lower left photograph is almost certainly looking in the opposite direction, or south, along Old Well Walk towards Grove Cottage, Montpellier, in the 1860s.

Above is the approximate line of Old Well Walk across the former Church Meadow, with the Ladies' College ahead and the Royal Well bus station behind (opened in 1936). The college was built over the Old Well and part of the magnificent (800–900ft) avenue of elm trees laid out between 1738 and 1742. The small car park ahead on St George's Road is where Royal Well Chapel stood until 1965.

Cheltenham Ladies' College (built 1873 onwards) with the fine French-style tower added in 1876. Royal Well Chapel (see previous page) is visible on the left edge of the top left picture. The next photograph was taken in Old Well Lane (renamed Montpellier Street in 1844) with St George's Road at the far end, where the far trees are in Royal Crescent Gardens (the old Church Meadow).

The first three pictures show the Principal's cottage, occupied by Miss Dorothea Beale from 1873 until its demolition in 1893. Picture four shows the cottage being demolished for the building of the college's Library Wing against Montpellier Street. During the next building phase (1895/7), the last (1849) Royal Old Well Pump Room was demolished for the building of the college's Princess Hall, being used for various college functions until then. While Miss Beale lived in the nearby cottage it is reasonable to assume she would have taken the waters there. The Pump Room was located just behind the photographer in the fourth picture where new building's footings are being prepared.

Lower left (1920s view) inside the college grounds, now with the Library Wing (right) attached to the Art and Music Wing (left) at the point where Miss Beale's cottage stood. The last picture, on the right (2010) shows little has changed since the 1890s extensions. Today the college has an impressive interpretation board in a corridor near the Princess Hall explaining the history of the former Royal Well, including a selection of early engravings of scenes of the functioning well and the 1788 royal visit. Today, only old maps and modern archaeology might reveal the footprint of the 1849/50 Royal Well Pump Room, and possibly the earlier (1739) Assembly Room and the later (1775/6) Assembly Room, all hidden somewhere beneath the modern college's floors, lawns and paths.

The octagonal Tudor Gothic style Cambray Spa was built at the junction of Oriel Road and Rodney Road in 1834. Its medicinal spring was described as 'pure chalybeate' and 'simple carbonated chalybeate'. On the 1860s carte de visite 'Aperient Saline and Chalybeate Spa' is written above the door. Sir Michael Faraday analysed its waters which were said to be as good as those in Tunbridge Wells. In 1873 it became a Turkish bath, the Victorians no doubt realising the curative and cleansing qualities of such bathing reached back to Roman times or earlier. By the 1830s hot vapour baths were believed beneficial for many ailments including inflammation of the bowels, bilious and liver complaints, diabetes, dropsy, gout, sciatica and rheumatism, cases of gravel and paralysis, all nervous disorders, dyspepsia and to aid circulation, etc. People no doubt bought into all this, readily believing such claims and we still seek remedies for most of these ailments. It was demolished in 1938.

The spa sat on the far side of this junction, partially inside the since widened Rodney Road, with the borough car park beyond. The River Chelt flows beneath this part of the town towards Royal Well and under the Promenade, re-emerging in St George's Place. In 1960 Rodney Road car park was the first in the country with its 6d in the slot 'Trust the Motorist' payment scheme. Following the demise of an earlier enterprise that charged for the free underground water, this canny scheme charged for previously free above-ground parking! It's not all bad news because a multi-storey car park was proposed for this location in 1975 but firmly rejected by the County Council.

The 1809 Alstone Spa was at the junction Great Western Road and Millbrook Street. Seen here in about 1910, its end wall reads, 'Cheltenham Saline Waters Supplied Direct From the Springs. Silver Medal, London 1906'. The last owner, George Ballinger (fruiterer and spa proprietor) ran it from the 1920s until 1939 after which his widow ran it until 1945. The small pump building was later removed and the adjoining house named Brooklyn occupied until redevelopment of the area in 2000. The still fairly new (1906) Cheltenham to Honeybourne branch railway line is behind the spa in this photograph.

This view exemplifies how developers are permitted to pay for a footbridge and less than lip-service to local heritage. Part of the 2000/3 £25m Costain/Waitrose development subsumed Great Western Road, and most of the original St James railway yard, renaming the new road and adjacent residences Honeybourne Way. Completed in 2003, today there is no acknowledgement to important chunks of Cheltenham's history that once existed here. The Honeybourne Cycle Track crosses over the new bridge but few people are aware that the bridge and roundabout are the only visual clues to Alstone Spa's location (1809–2000), the capped well-shaft lying ignominiously beneath the roundabout. A modest plaque would be an appropriate tribute to this little-known spa, not forgetting the ancient Upper Alstone Mill and Mill House (almost certainly one of ancient 'Chinteneha's' five Domesday mills in 1086) or Cheltenham's first Municipal Swimming and Water Polo Baths (1887–1975) or the two St James railway stations (1840–1966) underneath Waitrose. The company transforming this site espoused the importance of 'environmental impact' and you may judge for yourself if the claim gives due acknowledgement to this site's history.

From Great Western Road, photographer Ed Burrow seemed reluctant to raise his camera above the wall to photograph St James railway station! By this time (1900s) the original 1847 station had been extended eastwards in 1894 towards St Gregory's Church. The church on the right is St Matthew's in Clarence Street, its spire was removed in 1952 and the tower further lowered in 1972. St Mary's Parish Church spire is visible between them. The top inset photograph shows the GWR Cheltenham to Honeyborne line (1906–68) under construction from Great Western Road, with Alstone Spa top right (arrowed). The houses on the left are in nearby Great Western Terrace. The station was demolished in 1967.

With the wall demolished and gradient reduced, today you have to stand on the Honeybourne Cycle Track, west of the remodelled Honeybourne Way (former Great Western Road) to get the modern view of the site. Great Western Road can be seen in the inset aerial view, with Alstone Spa top left (arrowed). The roundabout at the bottom of Honeybourne Way (bottom picture) is Alstone Spa's former location. The old mill, baths, railway yard and other historic features lie below the new Waitrose development.

St James GWR railway station (1894–1966). The earlier (1840) station was further west (where Waitrose is today). The Gothic spire of St Gregory's Church (1857) is on the right. The tram is leaving for Lansdown Castle (giving its name to Holst's earliest work referring to an old toll-gate on Gloucester Road) via St George's Road and Gloucester Road. The large building beyond the station was the French Vice Consul's office in the 1850s. In these 1900s photographs it is Barnby Bendall's Furniture Repository.

After the railway station closed the area became a car park. In 1976/7 St James's House (left) was built for Mercantile & General. The former Barnby Bendall furniture repository more recently became a nightclub but is currently disused. Beyond this is the 1821 Christadelphian Hall.

Alstone Lower Mill, *c.* 1902. This mill was at the junction of Six Chimney Lane and Lower Mill Street (after Six Chimney Farm was renamed Arle Avenue in 1938). On the right is a former gasworks building. Tom Phillips, the miller, is on the sluice-gate bridge. Converted to steam power in the late nineteenth century, the mill closed in the 1920s after which the disused engine house and chimney stack were removed.

The author has added an arrow to the aerial photograph (*c.* 1930) to pinpoint the downstream mill. The gasworks building visible in the top photograph is above the mill in the aerial photograph. After the mill closed, Mill Cottages were owned by Cheltenham Skin Yard. Since the 1950s they have been owned by the Gas Club and restored. Behind the arrow, in the trees is Tudor Cottage, an ancient black and white timber-framed farmhouse. In 1929 it was carefully disassembled and rebuilt opposite Dowdeswell Reservoir at the entrance to Rossley Manor on the A40.

This 2010 comparison shot was taken from Gloucester Road Bridge because of inaccessibility downstream. The Environment Agency has upgraded the River Chelt's flow at historic pinch-points like this to improve its escape towards the River Severn, further reducing town centre flood risks.

Mr Stratford's Water Corn Mill at the east end of Capper's Pond (Pittville Lake) through which Wymans Brook formed the mill-race, *c.* 1900. For many years the brook carried Prestbury's untreated sewage to the River Severn; but even dirty water generated free energy that ground fine flour!

In 2010 a cleaner Wymans Brook overflows Marle Hill Lake in Pittville Park, washing over the remains of this important piece of Cheltenham's industrial archaeology. The former flour mill suffered the final ignominy of being ground into a rockery, where its foundation stones are easily spotted. The houses of more modern (1927) Hudson Street, St Pauls, and Cheltenham Recreation Centre (leisure@cheltenham), are visible through the trees.

Built between 1828 and 1848, Lansdown Crescent is one of the largest crescents in Britain, flourishing to the point that the 1841 census recorded one house with two male and six female servants. By the 1970s many apartments had succumbed to the ravages of time and an upsurge in demand for cheap bedsits accompanied by less than caring landlords, led to numerous squats and the dereliction that began to drag the crescent and surrounding area down, as I know only too well. Fortunately the decline was halted by the timely intervention of a tripartite rescue package between the Borough Council, central government and the Guinness Trust. The trust's lengthy programme of restoration and conservation pulled this beautiful convex crescent with its wrought- and cast-iron balconies back from the brink, setting the standard for similar rescue work elsewhere. Today it comprises a pleasant mixture of private and residential social landlord-owned properties.

This carte de visite image of Lansdown Crescent is unique in that we know exactly when it was taken – April 1864. It appears the photographer (or whoever commissioned him) thoughtfully included the horse-drawn carriage in this photograph and the one of the same date on p. 111.

Lansdown Place with canopied 'Bath-chairs' awaiting fare paying passengers, 1860s. Popular in spa towns, they superseded the sedan chairs, ten of which were licensed by Cheltenham Town Commissioners in 1810. In 1834 a sedan fare was 6*d* not exceeding 500 yards, 500–900 yards cost 1*s* and 900 yards to 1 mile would set you back 3*s*. Sedan chairs were phased out soon before these early street photographs were taken.

Two centuries later and benefiting from the Guinness Trust investment, straight-styled Lansdown Place forms part of a broad tree-lined road into Cheltenham from Gloucester, once thought of as the town's finest approach. Modern cars now clutter former front gardens.

Lansdown Parade was built between 1835 and 1838 between Lansdown Crescent and Douro Road. It is seen here on an 1860s carte de visite and has disproportionately large Greek Doric porches. The houses were initially occupied by Empire retirees – particularly members of the East India Company. Of nearby Lansdown Terrace, in 1926 the then Duke of Wellington remarked 'Lansdown Terrace just misses being one of the most interesting and successful designs for a row of houses ever made' – fair praise for much else on the Lansdown estate.

Within Regency Cheltenham, Lansdown Parade is much sought-after among the town's acclaimed period properties. It remains refreshingly intact, with permitted internal modifications and fittings reflecting current trends. Having spoken to some residents in this discreetly well-kept corner of Cheltenham, there is little doubt that the survival and preservation of these architectural gems is pivotal to the future reputation and standing of our historic town, whose modern owner/occupiers are doing all they can to hand these properties on to future custodians in the best possible shape. Classically proportioned dwellings like this still attract people from far and wide to enjoy a little of Cheltenham's amazing cultural heritage.

The General Hospital was Cheltenham's last important building in the Classical style. Built on Sandford Field it opened in 1849, replacing the 1839 Cheltenham Dispensary and Casualty Hospital at 318 High Street (Idmiston, now Normandy House). This 1860s carte de visite shows a wide sweep approach for horse-drawn carriages and ambulances and the town's last horse-drawn ambulance was bought in 1904. The hospital soon began to be enlarged and that programme continues.

The original General Hospital frontage is on the Sandford Road side of this large site. The twenty-first century finds it struggling to keep its original identity as all about it expands relentlessly into a vast, partially articulated network of wards, offices and modern departments of clinical excellence, with support facilities on this and other sites.

Part of this mid-twentieth-century aerial view shows two large detached houses left of the main building (lower right corner). The centre one was partly incorporated into West Block. Further left the house called Lindley was on the corner of College Road and Sandford Road (1860s–1977) serving as Cheltenham College's Music School from 1915. Planning permission is currently awaited for a multi-storey car park on the north-eastern side of the hospital to alleviate a 'chronic' shortage of car parking for staff and visitors.

Originally this building on St Margarets Road was the Boys' Orphan Asylum. It opened in 1867 taking in twenty boys from any locality or denomination. This 1860s carte de visite view of the building was no doubt taken soon after. It ceased being a boys' orphanage in 1956. The property to the right is St Margarets House which became Black & White Coaches' offices in the 1930s. It was destroyed by a German bomb in 1940, the orphanage suffering little more than broken windows.

In 1957, assisted by a £2,000 donation from Sir George Dowty, the former orphanage was leased from the council for a nominal rent. Renamed Dowty House it became a residential home for nineteen lady senior citizens. In 1960 the house was extended to thirty-seven bedrooms for men and women of retirement age, each resident having a single room, with washbasin and heating. There are two lounges, a large dining room and a garden for residents. The home provides normal and high dependency care, entertainment, keep-fit sessions, quizzes and outings. The thirty-seven residents are self-funded and local authority funded at a cost of £500 each per week. They are looked after by fifty full and part-time staff.

Any meaningful attempt to include numerous commercial and substantial private houses that were demolished would require a weighty volume in its own right. Here we will include just a couple of examples, with many others published elsewhere. This is the Rodney Hotel, Rodney Road, (in existence between the 1920s and the 1960s) representing one of some thirty Cheltenham hotels closed since the Second World War.

It was replaced with the similar but characteristically less substantial Rodney House, first occupied in 1968 by UCCA. In 1989 UCCA needed larger premises and moved to the newer Fulton House on the former St James railway station site in Jessop Avenue. Now called UCAS, they have since moved to New Barn Lane, occupying Rosehill (that replaced a large house of the same name), the former Gulf Oil building. Rodney House is currently occupied by Direct Marketing Agency (DMS).

This area was 'Canbry meade' in 1605, named after a local family. In 1802 it was a parcel of land sold by Cambray Farm in a field south of High Street called Cambray Meadow (to see it on a map go to: www.charlton-park-cheltenham.co.uk and view p. 7 of the e-book). By 1805 'an elegant mansion' called Cambray House was built with gardens that included the River Chelt and today's Rodney Road car park and this photograph dates from about 1900. In 1854 Cheltenham Ladies' College leased it when first admitting pupils, vacating the premises when their new college was built on Bayshill Road in 1873 and Cambray House was a boys' school until 1889. When it came back onto the market, Cheltenham Ladies' College bought it as a boarding house and overflow school where pupils were prepared for the college. It was known as 'Cambray House School', independent of the main college until they merged in 1914. In 1937 it was demolished and Cambray Court flats were built.

Cambray Court comprises fifty-six privately owned leasehold flats in three blocks on the edge of the River Chelt.

Suffolk Square was commenced in the 1820s and St James' Church was built between 1825 and 1830 in the Gothic Revival Style. This 1860s carte de visite shows the established front garden with sweeping carriage approach. Interestingly, the church clock shows 4.45 in both pictures, which I hope is a coincidence, as opposed to a century or more of faulty mechanism!

The terrace remains in good shape but the church was deconsecrated in 1976 and after that was used as a parish hall and sale room. It now finds itself 'converted' from a place of worship into a popular pizza restaurant, preserving this Regency masterpiece for anyone needing to satiate their culinary appetite, as opposed to their spiritual one.

The 1716 discovery of the Original or Old Well (Royal Well) eventually led to some twenty-six commercially run mineral wells in Cheltenham. In the century that followed, the grandest of them all was the Grecian styled Pittville Spa set in beautiful parkland. Pittville Spa and Pump Room (built between 1825 and 1830) was financed by Joseph Pitt as the focal point of his envisioned 100-acre Pittville Estate, on which he planned over 6 miles of rides and drives. Pitt never achieved his dream due to a downturn in banking and property ventures, but he did succeed in creating the finest specifically designed 'spa' building in England. This 1860s carte de visite captures a little of its grandeur with three carved Greek gods on the roof and three 'modern' Victorian girls on the lawns, in what remains Cheltenham's luxuriant oasis of tree-lined, gracefully bridged lakes and recreational parkland, still enjoyed by young and old alike.

Pittville Spa was purchased by Cheltenham Corporation in 1889. In 1915 the demand for Cheltenham waters nationally exceeded supply. Today, if your stomach is up to it, it is the only remaining spa at which you can experience the Cheltenham Waters.

At the end of the Second World War its future was in doubt. Threatened with dry rot and hampered by cost, its heritage value was recognised and despite post-war austerity, great sums were raised for its restoration. Having overcome challenging moments in its history, it ranks as the prime architectural jewel in Cheltenham's Regency crown, hosting many functions. These have included diverse events, some spilling out into the park, and wartime occupation by American troops and their stores, with less than graceful concrete-floored Nissen huts on the front lawn. That was when, anecdotally, the Bath stone figures (Aesculapius, Hygeia and Hippocrates) almost left their lofty perch and went west as English trophies, much as the town's last stagecoach did some fifteen years later (the coach left with a bill of sale!) Local craftsmen replaced the original eroded statues in the 1960s. Maintenance costs remain a challenge to its future but its

popularity for civil weddings, sales, auctions, exhibitions, meetings and dances should ensure its survival into the next century. The three Elizabethan (II) girls are Annabel, Sophie and Georgia – the last two being the author's granddaughters.

The Black & White Coach Company (1926–76) grew into Black & White Motorways Ltd, with an office at Paris House in the Promenade. Here we see its coaches in the 1930s. In 1931 they moved from Charlton Kings to St Margaret's Road, using St Margaret's House as a booking office until it was destroyed by a bomb in 1940. With roof-racked luggage, these open and canvas-covered buses more resemble a safari than a day-trip to London, adventurous as that must have been when so few people owned cars. In August 1950, 350 coaches and over 10,000 passengers passed through here in a single day.

The ongoing need for in-town car parking finds the site well used and a steady source of borough income. Other proposals have included new municipal offices, but not as yet!

Messrs Whitehead & Williams' new business was at 19 Portland Street in 1904 and soon after Alfred Williams (on the left) continued the business alone, Mr Whitehead opting for the motor trade. Britain didn't import bicycles then, manufacturing them all here. In 1990 Williams Cycles moved to larger premises in Albion Street where the business is run today by Alfred's grandson Andrew.

New businesses continue to start up in Cheltenham and in 1959 Roylan, in Suffolk Parade, was started by Cecil Glanville. Cecil's son-in-law, John, worked with him from the 1970s, taking over in the 1980s when Cecil retired. John retired in 2004 and his son Matthew now runs the business, stocking over 200 bicycles compared with a handful in the 1960s. Most are made in Taiwan, British bicycle manufacturing now being practically non-existent. Left to right are: Matthew (proprietor), John (Matthew's father), David (customer and author) Bob (Matthew's business partner) and Adrian (customer and local butcher).

The final word goes to the parish church dedicated to St Mary, now the oldest surviving building in Cheltenham. It was the only church here before the 1820s, after which many others were built. As far as is known, parts date from 1160–70, with much of it from about 1300 when it was extended. Its earliest parts probably stood here in the times of ancient 'Chintenaha', of the 1086 Domesday survey, built solidly upon the ghostly footprint of an eighth-century monasterium. It is possible that this 1860s carte de visite is the earliest photograph of Cheltenham's medieval mother church, which would have attracted the first photographers. In the lower right corner an earlier perpendicular porch is visible on the south-west transept – today's beautiful Prayer Chapel Window. This porch was removed during the 1859–61 Victorian restoration. In 1843 the tenor bell fell from a beam during an evening ringing and the bell ringers were lucky to escape uninjured, this being just one of countless fascinating stories attached to this beautiful building.

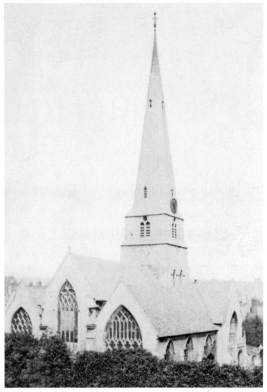

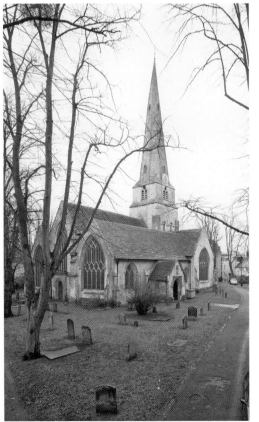

Today St Mary's Parish Church is one of five Grade I listed buildings in Cheltenham*. It is seen here with the 'newer' (c. 1890) Victorian gabled porch over another south-west window some 40ft to the left. While admiring Cheltenham's oldest building today we can use Google Earth's 3D-modeling. Having witnessed so many events and changes in Cheltenham it is now embracing the digital age and a greater contrast between ancient and modern is hard to find – one more significant milestone on its lengthy timeline and probably the best example yet of 'Cheltenham Past and Present'.

*others are: Pittville Pump Room, All Saints Church, Montpellier Rotunda and Thirlstaine House in Bath Road.

BIBLIOGRAPHY

Blake, Steven, *Cheltenham: A Pictorial History*, Phillimore & Co., 1996
Bradbury, Oliver, *Cheltenham's Lost Heritage*, Sutton Publishing, 2004
George Rowe's Illustrated Cheltenham Guide 1845, reprinted 1981
Griffith, S.Y., *History of Cheltenham*, 1838
Hart, Gwen, *A History of Cheltenham*, 1981
Heasman, Elaine, *Images of England, Cheltenham*, Tempus, 1998 and 2003
Hodsdon, James, *An Historical Gazetteer of Cheltenham*, Sutton Publishing, 1997
Little, Bryan, *Cheltenham in Pictures*, David & Charles, 1967
Martin, Colin, *Cheltenham's Trams & Early Buses*, Tempus, 2001
Osmond, Stephen, *A Chronology of Cheltenham*, 2000
Rowbotham, Sue & Waller, Jill, *Cheltenham A History*, 2004
Various bulletins of the Cheltenham Local History Society
Various directories and annuaires at Cheltenham Library